YORK NOTES

General Editors: Professor A.N. Jeffares (*University of Stirling*) & Professor Suheil Bushrui (*American University of Beirut*)

William Shakespeare

AS YOU LIKE IT

Notes by Charles Barber

MA (CAMBRIDGE) PH D (GOTHENBURG)
Formerly Reader in English Language and Literature, University of Leeds

YORK PRESS
Immeuble Esseily, Place Riad Solh, Beirut.

LONGMAN GROUP LIMITED
Burnt Mill,
Harlow, Essex

First published 1981
Second impression 1985
ISBN 0 582 78142 6

Produced by Longman Group (FE) Ltd
Printed in Hong Kong

Contents

Part 1

Introduction

The historical background

William Shakespeare lived from 1564 to 1616, during which time there was a period of relative stability and peace in English society. This period of calm occurred between two periods of tumult and change, the Reformation and the Civil Wars. The Reformation was the breaking-away of the English church from the authority of the Pope in Rome, followed by changes in doctrine and church services. It was started by King Henry VIII about twenty-five years before Shakespeare was born, and involved a period of conflict between Protestants (reformers) and Catholics (traditionalists) which broke out at times into armed rebellion, both under the Protestant King Edward VI (1547–53) and under the Catholic Queen Mary (1553–8). Twenty-five years after Shakespeare's death, England was just entering the Civil Wars (1640–9), the armed struggle between King and Parliament which can well be called the English Revolution.

The Reformation and the Civil Wars were major stages in the change from feudal England to capitalist England. In Shakespeare's lifetime, English society still had feudal forms and a feudal social structure, but within it there were powerful forces for change. There were puritans, who wished to carry the Reformation further and to abolish bishops; there were scientists, who were undermining traditional views of the universe; and above all there were capitalist landlords and merchants who, especially in south-eastern England, were trying to break down or evade the customary controls on economic activity.

The age of Shakespeare, then, was one both of stability and of tension, and both exercised a strong effect on his art. The period of relative calm and prosperity in the second half of the reign of Queen Elizabeth I (1558–1603) provided material conditions in which a professional English theatre could flourish; the social tensions provided, if only indirectly, the subject-matter for the greatest plays of this theatre.

The social hierarchy

In English society in Shakespeare's time there was a well-defined hierarchy, that is, a series of graded ranks. In theory, every individual belonged to one of these grades; and what he could do and could not do, and even the clothes he was permitted to wear, depended on the grade to which he belonged. Four main grades were usually recognised: (1) Gentlemen, (2) Citizens, (3) Yeomen, and (4) Artificers and Labourers. The second group, citizens, did not include everybody who worked in a town, but only those who were masters of their trade; it thus excluded journeymen (craftsmen hired by the masters, and paid a daily wage) and also apprentices. The third group, yeomen, were substantial farmers, who held land worth at least forty shillings a year; unlike gentlemen-landlords, they might engage in manual labour on their farms. The fourth group included all kinds of wage-labourers, and peasants who were not substantial enough to qualify as yeomen.

The first group, that of the gentlemen, was subdivided into a considerable number of grades. At the top was the prince (or sovereign); then came the peers or nobility (dukes, marquises, earls, viscounts, barons); and finally the lesser gentry (knights, esquires, gentlemen). It will be noticed that the word *gentleman*, which was of great importance in Shakespeare's England, had more than one meaning. It can mean anybody in the top group of society, including knights, noblemen, and even the monarch. But it was also used as the name of one sub-group of this class, namely the lowest, the simple gentleman.

The gentlemen (in the wide sense) probably constituted only about five per cent of the population, but they had almost all the power and many privileges. Essentially they were a landowning class, but certain other groups were also recognised as gentlemen, for example army officers of the rank of captain and above and men with a doctor's degree from a university (though there was always some dispute about the exact boundaries).

When we read Shakespeare, we have to remember that words like *gentle* and *noble* often refer to social status, as do words like *base*, *common*, *mechanic*, and *vulgar* (all of which refer to people of the lowest class). In the opening scene of *As You Like It*, one of Orlando's chief complaints against his brother is that he has not given him the education appropriate to a gentleman, and has thus undermined his gentle status. When, in the same scene, Orlando and Oliver engage in actual physical violence against each other, Oliver calls Orlando a villain, to which Orlando replies:

> 'I am no villain: I am the youngest son of Sir Rowland de Boys, he was my father, and he is thrice a villain that says such a father begot villains.' (I.1.53–5)

Here Orlando is playing on two meanings of *villain*: (a) scoundrel, criminal, (b) peasant, serf, low-born rustic. He means that Oliver is a scoundrel to say that the son of a knight is a peasant. The word *citizen*, similarly, refers specifically to one social group. In *As You Like It*, when

Jaques moralises over the stricken deer (II.1.45–63), he refers to the rest of the herd as 'fat and greasy citizens' who sweep pitilessly past the victim, the 'poor and broken bankrupt'. This is a satirical hit at the citizen-classes, suggesting that they are selfish and cynical, and abandon a fellow-citizen who runs into financial difficulties. The phrase *fat and greasy* suggests both the well-fed opulence of the citizens, and also the fact that their hands and clothes could be soiled by the handling of goods (whereas a gentleman did not engage in anything resembling manual labour, and was careful to keep his hands and his clothes clean).

In practice, the social system was more complicated than the four-class scheme suggests. Moreover, the class-barriers were not rigid, and there was movement both up and down. Indeed, in the sixteenth century there was a whole new nobility, created by the Tudor monarchs, alongside the ancient nobility, while many successful merchants and lawyers climbed into the ranks of the gentry. In *As You Like It*, Touchstone is perhaps referring to this situation when he tells of the knight who swore by his honour, but was not forsworn, because he had never had any (I.2.61–76). Despite the complications, however, the status of gentleman was a key one, and the reader of Shakespeare has to learn to respond to the implications of words like *gentle*.

The Elizabethan world-view

The dominant beliefs of the age reflect the hierarchical forms of society: the idea of order or hierarchy is central. The whole universe formed one vast hierarchy, from God down to the minerals; there were no gaps in the chain, and everything had a place in it. Below God were the angels, arranged in nine ranks; then human beings, arranged in social classes; then three grades of animal life; then vegetable life; and finally inanimate objects. Man was a key point in the chain, the link between matter and spirit, and he constituted a kind of miniature universe, a microcosm. There were detailed resemblances between his body and the universe. For example, the world was believed to be made of four elements (earth, air, fire, water), composed of pairs of four fundamental qualities (hot, cold, moist, dry). Similarly, a man's temperament (*complexion*) was thought to be determined by the balance within him of four fluids called humours (melancholy, blood, choler, phlegm), composed of the same four qualities. The hierarchies that composed the universe were similar to one another in various ways: as God was head of the universe, so the king was head of society, the lion was the king of beasts, the eagle the king of birds, the sun the chief of the heavenly bodies, the head the chief part of the human body, and so on.

According to traditional astronomy, the earth was at the centre of the universe. Surrounding the earth was a series of concentric transparent hollow spheres, which carried the heavenly bodies. Seven of the spheres carried the 'planets', which in order from the earth were the Moon, Mercury, Venus, the Sun, Mars, Jupiter, and Saturn; each of these spheres had its own proper rotation. Outside these was a sphere carrying the so-called fixed stars; and outside this a ninth sphere, the Primum Mobile, which rotated the whole system of nine spheres once every twenty-four hours. According to some authorities, each sphere as it rotated emitted a different musical note (inaudible to human ears), the resulting harmony being known as the Music of the Spheres – to which there is a reference in *As You Like It* (II.7.5–6). The lowest sphere, that of the Moon, separated our terrestrial world from the heavens. The sublunary world (the world below the sphere of the Moon) was composed of the four elements, and was subject to continual change. The elements were arranged in a hierarchy: the basest, earth, was at the centre; then came water; then air; and at the top came the noblest, fire (the region of comets and meteors). The heavens, above the sphere of the moon, were composed, not of the four elements, but of a fifth element, the quintessence or ether, which was perfect; the heavens were therefore perfect and unchanging. In Shakespeare's time this picture was already being challenged by advanced thinkers, but it remained the view of the ordinary educated man until the middle of the seventeenth century.

According to this world-view, it is natural for people to accept their place in the social hierarchy: it is natural (and therefore right) for subjects to obey their king, women to obey their husbands, children to obey their parents. The king is God's deputy on earth, and rebellion against him is rebellion against God, and therefore a sin. The doctrine of the Divine Right of Kings held that a monarch derived his authority from God, and was responsible only to him, not to his subjects.

Man's salvation

There were bitter religious disputes in sixteenth-century England, but it was still taken for granted that everybody in the country was a Christian and accepted a certain religious view of the universe. According to this view, the universe had a purpose: it had been created by God for the benefit of mankind, and it was the stage on which was enacted the drama of man's salvation. When God created the first human beings, Adam and Eve, and placed them in the Garden of Eden, they were perfect and sinless. Then came the Fall of Man: at the instigation of the serpent (identified by theologians with Satan), Adam and Eve disobeyed God and became sinful, and were expelled from the Garden of Eden. Without sin, mankind would have been immortal, but the result of sin is death. Moreover, sinfulness is inherited, so that all mankind (who are descended from Adam and Eve) are inherently sinful, and subject to death. After death, the soul lives on, and may be rewarded or punished by God. The punishment for sin is eternal damnation in Hell, but God has redeemed mankind from this punishment: he himself came to earth as a man, Jesus Christ, and suffered death by crucifixion, thus taking upon himself the punishment due to mankind. All those who believe in him are forgiven their sins, and will escape Hell, going instead to eternal bliss in Heaven. At the end of the world will come the Last Judgment (or Doomsday): God, surrounded by his angels, will descend to the earth; the dead will arise from their graves, and God will sit in judgment on every member of mankind.

The middle way of Queen Elizabeth I

The social and political conflicts of the age tended to be fought out in the arena of religion. At one extreme there were the puritans, who wished to push the Reformation further, and to remove from the church what they considered to be relics of paganism. At the other extreme there were the Catholics, who wanted to restore older forms of worship and once again recognise the Pope as the head of the English church. Catholicism was illegal in England in Elizabeth's reign, since Catholics did not recognise her as the legitimate queen; but it was still a strong force, especially in the more feudal north, while Puritanism was strongest in the south-east and in the great seaports. Between these extremes there was a whole spectrum of intermediate opinion.

Elizabeth maintained her position by constant compromise, and by holding the balance of power between the contending parties. Her policy of compromise is illustrated by her church settlement. It was still universally accepted that there could be only one church in England, compulsory for all; the disputes were about the nature of this church. Elizabeth's settlement tried to make the Church of England acceptable to as many people as possible. The monarch was head of the church, and it was governed by bishops, thus maintaining hierarchy; but many disputed points of doctrine were deliberately left ambiguous. From most of the population, Elizabeth demanded only an outward conformity, saying that she had no 'windows on men's souls'. The Church of England, not unnaturally, was attacked from both sides, Catholic and Puritan, but aimed at holding the central ground and conciliating the moderates in both camps.

In the 1580s, after some years of relative stability in England, there was a growing sense of national unity and national pride. These feelings were greatly encouraged by the events of 1588. In that year Spain, the most powerful of the Catholic countries, attempted to invade England with an army carried in an enormous fleet, the so-called Great Armada. The Armada was crushingly defeated by the English navy: of 129 ships that left Spain, only 54 battered wrecks limped home. But, what was perhaps more important, the expected Catholic revolt in England did not take place. Nobody knew how many secret Catholics there were in England, nor what percentage of them belonged to the militant wing that advocated armed rebellion. But the ruling classes certainly feared such a revolt, and it was this fear that led many puritans and many capitalist landlords to support the crown. When the Spanish fleet sailed up the English Channel, many people expected a major uprising; but in the event the Catholic rebellion just did not materialise; and the euphoria of the years following 1588, the exhilaration and the sense of national unity, were surely due as much to this fact as to the defeat of the Armada.

The equilibrium of the 1590s

But the moment of national unity contained the seeds of its own decay. If there was no longer any danger of a Catholic counter-revolution, there was no longer any need for puritans or capitalist gentry to support the crown: and the stage was set for the coming conflict between king and parliament. But for ten or fifteen years there was an uneasy truce, partly because of the long war against Spain, partly because many men were content to wait for the old queen to die, hoping for new policies from her successor. So there was a period of balance or equilibrium, like the interval between an ebbing and a flowing tide. Then, in the early years of the seventeenth century, social forces became more and more polarised, and the struggle began between crown and parliament, to culminate in the Civil Wars.

It will be seen that Shakespeare's career as a dramatist, which ran from about 1590 to 1612, came at a critical point in English history. The first decade of his writing occurred in the upsurge of national confidence and exhilaration which followed the defeat of the Armada, when class-conflicts were temporarily damped down and there was a strong sense of national unity. In the theatre, these feelings are reflected in the popularity of history plays, which usually handle the events of England's past in a patriotic manner; they are a common theatrical type until about 1605, after which time they almost entirely disappear. Even more popular were comedies, which were the commonest theatrical type on the English stage throughout the 1590s. Shakespeare's plays up to 1600 conform to this pattern: he wrote nine history plays and about the same number of comedies, but only three tragedies. The history plays can be seen as a celebration of national unity and peace, depicting the horrors of the civil wars of the fifteenth century and looking forward to the unity and prosperity of Shakespeare's own time. The romantic comedies can be seen as celebrations of the English community in

Shakespeare's time in all its variety and robustness; although they contain critical and satirical elements, they are not satirical comedies, but festive and joyous ones; they are optimistic plays, with a faith in human nature and in the community. *As You Like It* belongs to this phase of Shakespeare's career. But in about 1600, when England begins to move into a period of crisis and conflict, Shakespeare's work shows a marked change: between about 1600 and 1608, the majority of his plays are tragedies, and even the plays which are nominally comedies are in fact really problem plays, quite unlike the romantic comedies of the 1590s. In the plays of this period, Shakespeare explores the growing social crisis of the time, not directly, but through ideas, attitudes, conflicting world-views.

The Elizabethan drama

Shakespeare was not an isolated phenomenon: he was the greatest figure in a theatrical industry which employed dozens of writers and produced hundreds of plays. Even if Shakespeare had never lived, the period from 1585 to 1625 would still have been a great age of English drama. The basis for this achievement was the existence in London of a number of permanent theatres and theatrical companies, and a large audience for them. The theatres performed every afternoon except Sunday, and put on a different play every day: a new play was not given a continuous run, but was revived for single performances, the intervals between revivals getting greater as its popularity declined. The standards of performance were high: the London theatre was a full-time professional theatre and its actors were famous all over northern Europe.

The first two specially-constructed public theatres in London, the Theatre and the Curtain, were built in 1576. At that time Shakespeare was twelve years old, and by the time he reached manhood the London theatre was an established institution, with its companies, its audiences, its conventions – an institution sufficiently stable and respectable to attract to its services an ambitious young man from the provinces with literary inclinations.

The theatres built in 1576 did not spring up suddenly out of nothing: there was already a centuries-old tradition of popular drama in England – religious plays, folk-festival plays, popular stage romances, moral plays with allegorical characters. Alongside these arose in the sixteenth century a more learned drama: at schools and universities students performed plays by Latin authors (Terence, Plautus, Seneca), and then English plays in imitation of them. There were also various kinds of elaborate entertainment at court, and by the 1580s elegant and stylish prose comedies were being performed by boy-companies at the court of Elizabeth I. So in the second half of the sixteenth century there was a profusion of dramatic traditions in England – religious and secular, popular and polite, academic and courtly.

One consequence of the period of national unity and social equilibrium in the 1580s and 1590s was that the theatre became genuinely national, addressing itself to all classes of society. University men went into the popular theatre as writers, and brought about a fusion of the popular and academic and courtly traditions. An example of this is Christopher Marlowe (1564–93), who went to the University of Cambridge, taking his B.A. degree in 1584 and his M.A. in 1587; he then wrote a series of famous and successful dramas for the London theatre,

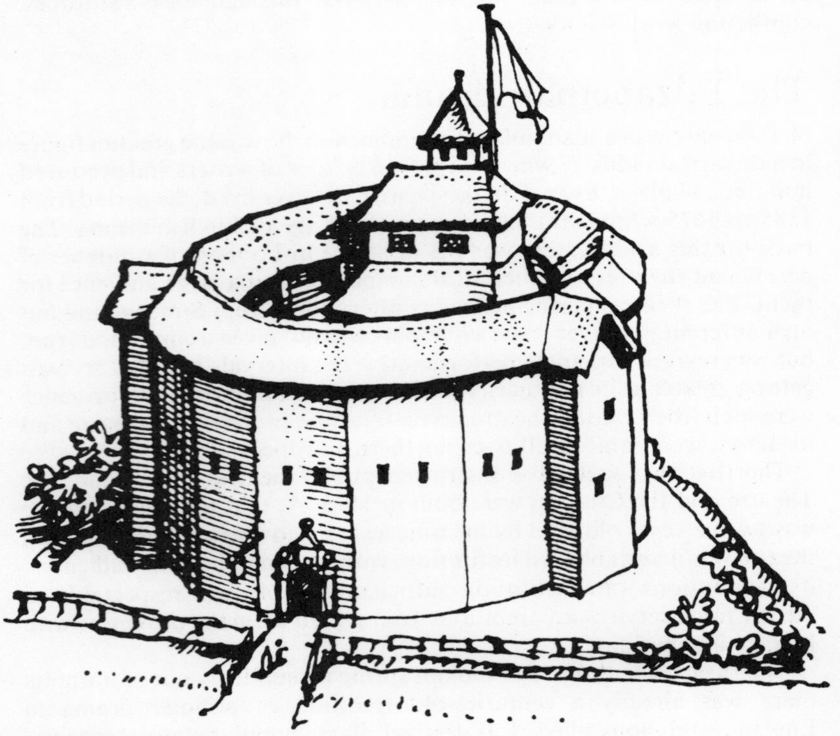

THE GLOBE PLAYHOUSE

The theatre, originally built by James Burbage in 1576, was made of wood (Burbage had been trained as a carpenter). It was situated to the north of the River Thames on Shoreditch in Finsbury Fields. There was trouble with the lease of the land, and so the theatre was dismantled in 1598, and reconstructed 'in an other forme' on the south side of the Thames as the Globe. Its sign is thought to have been a figure of the Greek hero Hercules carrying the globe. It was built in six months, its galleries being roofed with thatch. This caught fire in 1613 when some smouldering wadding, from a cannon used in a performance of Shakespeare's *Henry VIII,* lodged in it. The theatre was burnt down, and when it was rebuilt again on the old foundations, the galleries were roofed with tiles.

of which the best known is *Dr Faustus* (c. 1592). The fusion of traditions was possible because there was also a fusion of audiences: the theatre that Shakespeare wrote for represented all the classes of London, from noblemen down to labourers, and their womenfolk. And when Shakespeare's company performed for the Queen at court, they acted for her the same plays as they performed for the audience of their public theatre.

With the fusion of traditions, the great period of the English drama begins. The broad audience was a source of strength. For maximum success, plays needed the sophistication and elegance demanded by the gentry in the audience, but also the directness of appeal and the entertainment-value demanded by the uneducated. The fact that the best dramatists of the age could fulfil these requirements suggests that the different social groups in the audience had a remarkable community of outlook and interests.

But, like the equilibrium in society, the wide audience of Shakespeare's theatre was the product of just one moment in history, and then passed away. In the opening years of the seventeenth century, the single broad audience of the 1590s began to split into two audiences: a courtly audience at the more expensive indoor theatres, and a more popular audience at the old public theatres. Shakespeare's theatre, the Globe, with its great prestige, probably managed to retain a broad audience until the end of his theatrical career. But within a few years of his death the old public theatres had sunk to crude and noisy places where simple entertainment was given for the artisan classes, while specially-built indoor theatres catered for people of the highest rank and fashion. Under the influence of the rising tide of puritanism, the middle section had dropped out of the audience, leaving a plebeian audience on the one hand and an aristocratic audience on the other. Such different theatres demanded very different kinds of plays, and the synthesis of learned, popular, and courtly traditions gradually disintegrated.

The Elizabethan public theatre

The public theatres for which most of Shakespeare's plays were written were small wooden open-air theatres, in which the plays were performed by daylight. The width of a theatre was as great as its length: it could be round, or square, or octagonal, but not oblong. The Fortune Theatre (built in 1600) was eighty feet square outside, and fifty-five feet square inside, and this was probably a typical size. A theatre consisted of three tiers of galleries perpendicularly above one another, covered with a roof, surrounding an open central arena. From one side, the main stage projected halfway into the arena, partly protected from the weather by a roof supported at the front by two posts. These posts could be used in the action, and in *As You Like It* were probably used as trees on which Orlando hung his love-poems (III.2.1–10). The actors came on to the stage through large doors on each side of the back wall. They were very close to the audience, which was on three sides of the stage. Some spectators stood in the arena, while others had seats in the galleries. For obvious technical reasons there was no front curtain to the large projecting stage, so scenes began and ended simply by the entry and exit of the characters. Since the stage was large, a character who entered in the middle of a scene might take quite a time to reach the characters already on-stage: in the opening scene of *As You Like It,* Adam and Orlando are conversing when Oliver enters, but they have nineteen words of dialogue (unheard by Oliver) before he reaches them and addresses Orlando (I.1.24–6). In the back wall behind the main stage was a small inner stage concealed by curtains; here a character could hide and spy on others, or the curtains could be opened to reveal people or things hitherto concealed from the audience. In *As You Like It*, Amiens orders a table to be laid ready for a 'banquet' for the Duke (II.5.28–9, 59–60); the table was perhaps laid in the inner stage, and then concealed until two scenes later, when the Duke and his followers have a table with food on (II.7.88–106). Above this inner stage, at the level of the middle tier of audience galleries, was an upper stage which could be used to represent a balcony, or an upstairs window, or the walls of a town.

Elizabethan theatres made little use of scenery. Portable furniture, like chairs and tables, could be carried on to the stage, and sometimes a bed was pushed on; but no attempt was made to construct realistic sets. In *As You Like It* the Forest of Arden, with its trees and running brooks, its rows of osiers, its herds of deer, its sheepcote fenced about with olive-trees, is created for the audience by Shakespeare's writing, not by the carpenter or scene-painter. Since the performances were in daylight, no use was made of lighting-effects, and if the dramatist wished the audience to imagine that it was dark night, or brilliant sunshine, or storm, he had to achieve his effect by means of his words. On the other hand, the theatre did make considerable use of sound-effects and of music (such as the songs in *As You Like It*), and of splendid costumes (which were usually Elizabethan ones, with no attempt at historical accuracy). Predominantly, however, the theatre depended on the spoken word: it was a word-centred and actor-centred drama.

Because of the absence of scenery and of a front curtain, the action of the play could flow continuously without any break between the scenes, like a film. As the actors walked off the stage at the end of one scene, another group of actors came in by a different door for the next one. It is not necessary for a scene to take place in a clearly defined location: if the audience needs to know the location, it will be indicated by the speakers

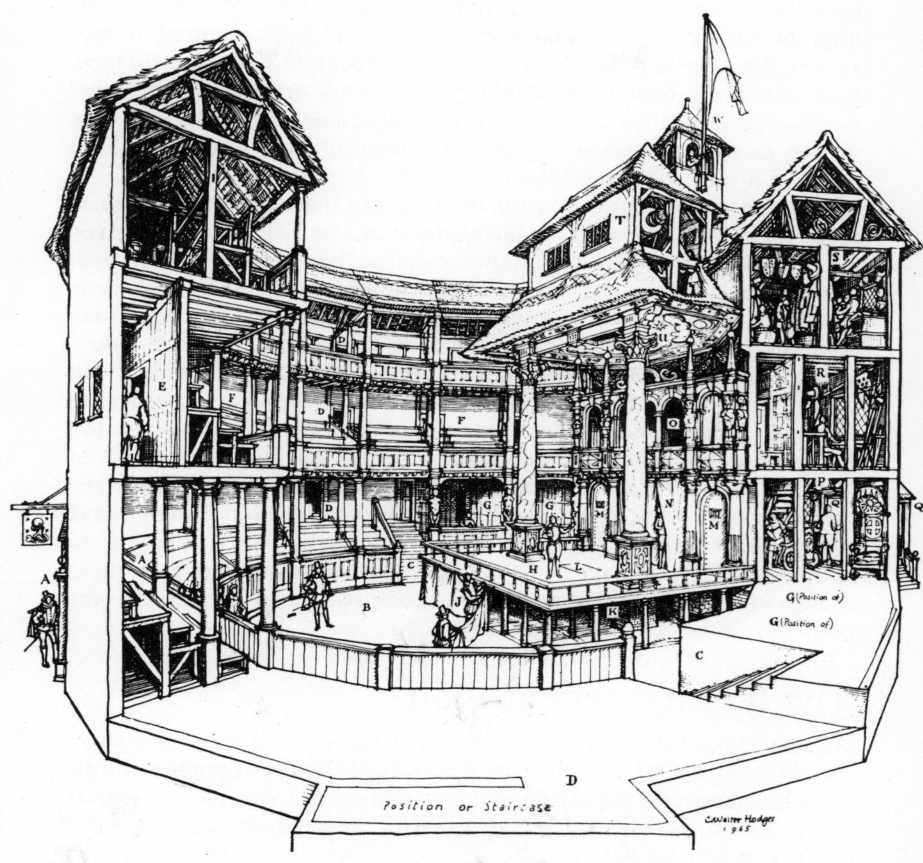

A CONJECTURAL RECONSTRUCTION OF THE INTERIOR OF THE GLOBE PLAYHOUSE

AA Main entrance
B The Yard
CC Entrance to lowest gallery
D Entrance to staircase and upper galleries
E Corridor serving the different sections of the middle gallery
F Middle gallery ('Twopenny Rooms')
G 'Gentlemen's Rooms' or Lords' Rooms'
H The stage
J The hanging being put up round the stage
K The 'Hell' under the stage
L The stage trap, leading down to the Hell
MM Stage doors
N Curtained 'place behind the stage'
O Gallery above the stage, used as required sometimes by musicians, sometimes by spectators, and often as part of the play
P Back-stage area (the tiring-house)
Q Tiring-house door
R Dressing-rooms
S Wardrobe and storage
T The hut housing the machine for lowering enthroned gods, etc., to the stage
U The 'Heavens'
W Hoisting the playhouse flag

(as in *As You Like It* II.4.12–13); but often there is no indication. Some modern editions of the plays give a location at the beginning of each scene ('Act I Scene 1. An orchard near Oliver's house'); but most of these stage-directions have been added by modern editors and are not found in the original editions. Time, too, may be compressed or stretched: in *As You Like It* an interval of over two hours is filled by Act IV Scene 2, a scene of a mere nineteen lines.

The treatment of time and the treatment of place are to be reckoned among the conventions of the Elizabethan theatre, for all drama rests on unstated assumptions which the audience has to accept. Another convention is that characters can speak in verse, as they frequently do in *As You Like It*. Other common conventions are the aside and the soliloquy. In the aside, we have to accept that a character can make a speech (or part of a speech) which is heard by the audience but not by the other characters on the stage; it is a way of revealing what a character is thinking. In the soliloquy, the character is alone on the stage, and utters his thoughts aloud for the audience to hear; it is moreover one of the conventions that, in a soliloquy, the character speaks the truth and reveals himself as he really is. There are also convention of plot and of action. An obvious one in *As You Like It* is the convention of the effectiveness of disguise: we have to accept that Rosalind merely has to change into man's clothes in order not to be recognised by the man who loves her and even by her own father.

The literary background

However broad the audience of the public theatre, the men who wrote the plays for it were usually men of education. Shakespeare himself did not go to a university, but he almost certainly went to a grammar school, and it is clear from his work that, while not a scholar, he was steeped in the learning of his time.

By the late sixteenth century, English education was dominated by the ideas of the humanists, ideas which had arisen in Italy in the late Middle Ages and gradually spread to northern Europe. Renaissance humanism was the belief in a certain type of education, namely one based on the pagan classics – the poetry, drama, oratory, history, and philosphy of ancient Greece and Rome. In practice it was Roman civilisation that was dominant. In Elizabethan grammar schools, the pupils were taught to read and write classical Latin (the literary language of Rome in the first century BC), and also to speak it. They read Latin authors, with especial emphasis on poetry, and were taught to analyse literary texts by the methods of classical rhetoric. Rhetoric was the art of oratory, speech-making, but even in antiquity its methods and procedures had been carried over to literature, and in the Renaissance the handbooks of rhetoric were commonly regarded as handbooks for poets. The pupils were also taught some elementary logic, based on that of Aristotle, the ancient Greek philosopher who was a major influence on European thought in the Middle Ages and Renaissance; and logic, like rhetoric, was applied to the techniques of reading and writing literature. In *As You Like It*, Touchstone in particular shows familiarity with the techniques of logical argument.

When university men began to write for the public theatres in the 1580s, this classical influence entered the popular drama. It is seen in such things as the structure of plays (for example the five-act pattern inherited from Roman comedy); in the free use of classical allusions, especially allusions to classical mythology (the legendary stories of gods and ancient heroes); in the taking over of stock characters from Roman dramatists (the tyrant, the parasite, the braggart, the clever witty servant); and in the influence of classical rhetoric on style.

William Shakespeare

Shakespeare was born in 1564 in Stratford-on-Avon, a small market town in the West Midlands. His father, John Shakespeare, came from a family of yeomen outside Stratford, but had moved into the town and become a glover, eventually owning his own shop. He prospered, bought property, and was elected to various civic offices; and in 1568–9 he was Bailiff, the chief civic dignitary of Stratford. We know nothing of William's boyhood, but there can be little doubt that, as the son of a prosperous citizen, he went to Stratford Grammar School, which was a good school and free for the sons of Stratford burgesses. In 1582 he married Anne Hathaway, a yeoman's daughter, by whom he had three children.

Apart from his christening, his marriage, and the birth of his children, we have no firm knowledge of Shakespeare's life until 1592, when an attack on him in a pamphlet by Robert Greene shows that he was already a dramatist of some reputation in London. His earliest plays date from about 1590, and he probably went to London and became an actor there not long before that date. For Shakespeare was not like the university men who wrote for the theatre without belonging to it: he was an actor and a professional man of the theatre, and it was on the success of a theatrical company that his fortunes were founded. His plays were doubtless a great asset to his company, but it was his position as a 'sharer' in the outstanding theatrical company of the day that made him a man of substance.

London theatrical companies were organised on a co-operative basis: a number of actors (the sharers) invested jointly in the necessary equipment (books, properties), hired a theatre, and shared the proceeds after each performance. The sharers, who would number between eight and twelve, played the major roles themselves, but they also hired journeymen actors, and for the women's parts they had boys, who had the status of apprentices; there were no actresses in Shakespeare's time. For legal reasons each company needed the patronage of some great nobleman, whose name it took; but in fact the companies were independent commercial organisations.

In 1594 there was a regrouping of the London theatrical companies after a severe plague, and Shakespeare and seven other actors joined forces to form a new company, the Lord Chamberlain's Men, which rapidly became the leading company of the time, with Richard Burbage as its outstanding performer. In 1599, Shakespeare was one of a consortium of investors who built the famous Globe Theatre, which became the normal home of the Chamberlain's Men. In 1603, when James I came to the throne, he took the company under his own patronage, and changed its name to the King's Men. Besides enjoying enormous success with the public, the company was invited more often than any other to perform at court before the sovereign during the Christmas revels and similar festivities, and Shakespeare's plays were often performed on these occasions.

As, after 1594, the Chamberlain's Men established themselves as London's leading company, so Shakespeare established himself as its leading playwright. In the early part of his career he wrote about two plays a year, mostly history plays and comedies, and in these he achieved a brilliant synthesis of the popular, academic, and courtly traditions. After 1600 he wrote rather less, not much more than one play a year; these later plays were mainly tragedies, until the very end of his career, when he wrote the so-called romances. In about 1612 he retired from the London theatre and returned to Stratford, where he was now rich enough to buy the best house in the town. He died in 1616.

Elizabethan English

The English language in Shakespeare's time differed in many ways from the English spoken today, and some of these differences affect the student of Shakespeare. There are differences in vocabulary, in pronunciation, and in grammar, and something will be said about each of these, with illustrations from *As You Like It*.

Vocabulary

Some words used by Shakespeare have since fallen out of use, and many more have changed in meaning since his time. Explanations of some of these words are given in Part 2 below. There are many such words, however, that occur more than once in the play, and to avoid repetitiveness in Part 2 their meanings are instead given here: **again** back; **an, an if** if; **anatomize** dissect, analyse; **and, and if** if; **atomies** motes, specks of dust; **ay** yes; **become** befit, suit; **beholding** beholden, indebted; **bid** invite; **burden, burthen** refrain (of a song); **cote** cottage; **countenance** demeanour, behaviour; **coz** cousin, relative; **cross** trouble, adversity; **deceived** mistaken; **disable** disparage, belittle; **dishonest** unchaste; **divers** different, various; **ere** before; **erewhile** recently; **erst** formerly; **even** straight, harmonious; **fain** glad(ly), willing(ly), compelled; **fall** let fall; **fancy** love, imagination; **fantasy** imagination, caprice, desire; **favour** facial appearance; **foil** throw (in wrestling); **fond** foolish; **foul** ugly, dirty, morally corrupt; **giddiness** flightiness, rashness; **giddy** frivolous, inconstant; **God buy you** God be with you, goodbye; **hence** from here; go away; **honest** chaste; **honesty** chastity; **humorous** moody, capricious; **humour** temperament, mood, whim; **'ild** reward; **ill-favoured** ugly; **learn** teach; **lief** gladly, willingly; **like** please; **modern** ordinary, everyday, commonplace; **naught** bad; **nay** no, well then; **occasion** opportunity, cause, pretext; **'ods** God's (in oaths); **o'er** over; **of** by, from; **out** at a loss, nonplussed; **passing** extremely; **peace** be quiet!; **policy** scheming, stratagem, intrigue; **presently** immediately; **prithee** (I) pray you, please; **proper** handsome, good-looking; **purgation** the clearing of oneself from accusation or suspicion; **question** conversation, discussion; **quoth** said; **rail** chide, utter abusive language; **rank** corrupt, gross, stinking, luxurious(ly); **rude** harsh, rough, turbulent; **sad** serious, solemn; **sans** without; **saw** saying, maxim; **show** appear, seem; **so** provided that; **soft** wait a moment, not so fast!; **still** always, continually; **straight** immediately; **suddenly** quickly, immediately; **ta'en** taken; **take up** make up, reconcile; **tax** accuse, criticise; **taxation** fault-finding, censoriousness; **taxing** criticism; **want** lack, be without; **withal** with, with it, moreover; **yond** that, the one over there.

Many of these words also occur in more familiar senses: for example, *again* and *and* occur frequently throughout the play with their present-day meanings.

Pronunciation

For the student of Shakespeare's plays, the major differences in pronunciation are those that affect the rhythm of the verse. Some words had a different stress-pattern from the one used today. The following words in *As You Like It* had the main stress on the second syllable: allies, aspect, compact (noun), confines (noun), contents (noun), envy (verb), persever, revenues. On the other hand, *antique* was stressed on the first syllable.

Many words could have one more stressed syllable than they have today: *pilgrimage* could have a stress on the third syllable as well as the first, and in that case it rhymes with *age* (as it does in *As You Like It*, III.2.126). Some words could not only have one more stress than today, but also one more syllable. For example, words ending in *-tion* could have an additional stress on the last syllable, and in that case the ending consisted of two syllables, not one, being pronounced *-si-on*. The following is an example from *As You Like It*:

'Where none will sweat, but for promotion.'

(II.3.60)

Here the word *promotion* has four syllables (*pro-mo-si-on*), with stresses on the second and fourth. Other words in *As You Like It* which have this type of pronunciation are condition (I.2.253), description (IV.3.85), function (II.7.79), intermission (II.7.32), observation (II.7.41), patience (I.3.76), and reputation (II.7.153). On the other hand, all such words could equally well have the present-day style of pronunciation, so that the poet could choose whichever suited his metre.

The verb-ending *-ed* was sometimes pronounced as a syllable in positions where today it is not, as in the following line:

'And they that are most galled with my folly.'

(II.7.50)

Here the *-ed* of *galled* must be pronounced, giving the word two syllables.

Grammar

There are many small differences of grammar between Elizabethan English and present-day English, but we need consider only those which can seriously affect meaning or may puzzle the modern reader.

In addition to the pronoun *you* there was another second-person pronoun *thou* (accusative *thee*, possessive *thine*): it was possible to say either *you walk* or *thou walkest*. In the plural, only *you* could be used: it has never been possible to use *thou* as a plural. In the singular, however, there was a choice between *you* and *thou*. *You* was the polite form, used to a social superior, or by a child to its parent; among the upper classes, it was also the normal form to a social equal. *Thou* could be used to a social inferior, a child, an animal; it was also the normal form used by members of the lower classes when addressing one another. *Thou* could also be used for emotional effect: among upper-class people on friendly terms, it marked affection or intimacy; but to a stranger it was insulting or hostile. For historical reasons, it was also customary (contrary to what might be expected) to address God as *thou*; and it was also normal to use *thou* to a pagan god or goddess, or an abstraction, or a personified inanimate object; in *As You Like It*, Orlando addresses the moon-goddess as *thou* (III.2.2). The social use of *thou* is seen in the conversations between Orlando and Adam: most often, Orlando addresses Adam as *thou*, while Adam replies with *you*. The hostile use of *thou* is seen in the conversation between Orlando and Oliver in the first scene of the play: they both begin by using the polite *you* (Oliver somewhat ironically), but when they become angry and grapple physically they both switch to the insulting *thou*. The intimate use of *thou* can be seen in the conversations between Rosalind and Celia: they fluctuate between *you* and *thou*, sometimes being neutral and sometimes more affectionate. Touchstone often acts the part of the great courtier patronising the country bumpkins, and so addresses Corin or William as *thou*.

Today, if there is no other auxiliary in the sentence, we form negatives and most questions by inserting the auxiliary *do*: we turn *You know* into *You do not know* or *Do you know*?. Shakespeare also used these forms, but equally well he could say *You know not* or *Know you?*, without using *do*. Moreover, he could insert *do* in affirmative statements, and say *I do know*; and the thing to be noticed here is that the *do* is not stressed, and does not signal sentence-emphasis (as it would today). So Jaques says:

'As I do live by food, I met a fool.'

(II.7.14)

Here, *I do live* is merely another way of saying *I live*, and must be spoken with the word *do* quite unstressed.

In verbs, there were two alternative endings for the third person singular in the present tense, *-(e)th* and *-(e)s*, as in he *walketh* or *walks*, *he passeth* or *passes*, *he hath* or *has*. By Shakespeare's time, the *-(e)s* forms were normal in everyday speech, while the *-(e)th* forms were rather literary and formal. When *thou* was the subject, the verb had the ending *-(e)st*, as in *thou knowest* or *knowst*; notice also the special forms *thou wilt*, *shalt*, *art* ('you will, shall, are'). In the second and third person singular of the present tense, the subjunctive was still commonly used: alongside *he walks* (or *walketh*) and *thou walkest* we find the subjunctive forms *he walk* and *thou walk*; and alongside *he is* and *thou art* we find the subjunctive forms *he be* and *thou be*. In subordinate clauses, the use of the subjunctive indicated doubt, uncertainty, unreality; it is therefore especially common after such conjunctions as *if* and *although* and *unless*, as in *if he come in* (I.1.123), *unless thou entreat for her* (IV.3.73). In main clauses, the subjunctive is used to express a wish, as in *Hercules be thy speed* 'may Hercules help you' (I.2.197). In the present-tense plural, the form with no ending was normal, like *they walk*; but it was also possible to use forms like *they walks* and *they walketh*. Such forms occur occasionally in Shakespeare; an example of the *-(e)s* plural in *As You Like It* is *Or as the Destinies decrees* (I.2.98).

The past tenses and past participles of verbs are often different from the forms which are standard today. Examples in *As You Like It* include *broke* 'broken', *forgot* 'forgotten', *shaked* 'shaken', *spoke* 'spoken', and *writ* 'wrote'.

The perfect tense, which today is formed with *have* and the past participle, was sometimes formed instead with *be* and the past participle, as in *Are you crept hither?* 'Have you sneaked in here?' (I.2.144–5) and *he is but even now gone hence* 'he has just this moment gone away' (II.7.3). The perfect with *be* could be used only with verbs of motion (like *come*) and with verbs of change of state (like *become*). When it was used, it focused attention on the outcome of the action denoted by the verb, not on the action itself.

Until about 1600, the word *its* did not exist. The possessive form of *it* was *his*, as when Jaques says that the old man's voice *whistles in his sound* (II.7.164). The use of *his*, therefore, does not imply personification.

In a negative sentence, it was possible to use two (or even more) negative words, as when Celia says *I cannot go no further* (II.4.8). The two negatives do not cancel one another out; on the contrary, they reinforce one another, making the negation even more emphatic.

In the comparison of adjectives, the Elizabethans could use either *-er, -est* or *more, most*, but had more freedom of choice than we have today: for example, they could say either *most famous* or *famousest* (whereas today only the former is possible). They could also combine the two methods of comparison, as when Touchstone says *more sounder* (III.2.58) and *more worthier* (III.3.54).

A note on the text

In 1623, seven years after Shakespeare's death, some of his former colleagues published his collected plays in one large folio volume. This edition is called the Shakespeare First Folio (F1 for short), and is our sole authority for about half of his plays, including *As You Like It.* A number of the plays had been published individually in his lifetime, but this was not true of *As You Like It*, for which F1 is the only authoritative source. The text of *As You Like It* in F1 appears to be a good one, and the printers probably set it from a playhouse prompt-copy, or from a transcription of a prompt-copy specially made for publication. There are no signs of serious textual corruption, though there are some confusions between verse and prose, which are normally straightened out by modern editors. The Act and Scene divisions look correct, except that a new scene should probably begin after III.2.10: the stage is empty after Orlando's exit at that point, and in Shakespeare's theatre an empty stage is precisely the mark of a scene-ending. Moreover, Orlando hangs his poems up by night (he addresses the moon), whereas what follows obviously takes place by day.

Different editions of *As You Like It* will be found to have somewhat different line-numbers. This is because the play contains many prose passages, and these obviously occupy different numbers of lines of print in different editions. It is therefore necessary to give line-numbers from one particular edition, and for these Notes the edition chosen is a cheap and easily available paperback, in the New Penguin series:

William Shakespeare, *As You Like It*, edited by H. J. Oliver, Penguin Books, Harmondsworth, 1968.

If you use a different edition, you should have no difficulty in identifying passages referred to, since the numbering is seldom likely to differ by more than about ten lines.

Part 2

Summaries
of AS YOU LIKE IT

A general summary

Orlando de Boys has been left a mere thousand crowns in his father's will, the bulk of the estate having gone to Orlando's eldest brother, Oliver. But Oliver withholds the money from Orlando, and also refuses to provide him with the education suitable for a gentleman, despite their father's last instructions. Orlando quarrels with Oliver, and demands his thousand crowns. Oliver plans to get rid of him by having him killed in a wrestling match, which takes place before Duke Frederick and his court. Orlando, however, defeats the professional wrestler who has been incited to kill him. Adam, an old family servant, warns Orlando not to return to Oliver's house, since Oliver is planning his murder. Adam offers Orlando his life's savings, and the two of them go off to seek their fortune elsewhere.

At the wrestling, Orlando had met two princesses: Celia, Duke Frederick's daughter, and Rosalind, his niece; Orlando and Rosalind had been deeply attracted to one another. Rosalind is the daughter of the former duke, Duke Senior, who had been deposed some years previously by his younger brother Frederick, and who is now living with some of his followers in the Forest of Arden. Hitherto, Duke Frederick has permitted Rosalind to remain at court, because of Celia's affection for her; now, however, he accuses her of treason, and banishes her. Celia is unwilling to be parted from Rosalind, and they run away together in disguise to look for Duke Senior in the Forest of Arden: Rosalind dresses as a boy, and takes the name of Ganymede, while Celia dresses as a girl of humble rank and takes the name of Aliena; they persuade Duke Frederick's fool, Touchstone, to accompany them. When their disappearance is discovered, Duke Frederick suspects that they have gone off with Orlando; he questions Oliver, seizes his estate, and instructs him to find Orlando and bring him back within a year.

In the Forest of Arden, Duke Senior and his followers are leading a contented pastoral life. One of his followers is Jaques, who affects melancholy and makes satirical comments on everything. Orlando and Adam arrive in Arden, and join the Duke and his followers. Celia, Rosalind, and Touchstone also arrive in Arden; Celia buys a sheep-farm, and they live there. There are various encounters of wit between Touchstone and Jaques, Orlando and Jaques, and others. Orlando hangs poems in praise of Rosalind on trees in the forest. Rosalind and Celia (still in disguise) meet him; Rosalind/Ganymede undertakes to cure him of his love: he must pretend that Ganymede is his love Rosalind, and woo him under her name; Ganymede will respond like a fickle and capricious woman, and so bring Orlando to his senses. Orlando, who just wants to think and talk about Rosalind, agrees to do this. Silvius, a young shepherd, loves Phebe, a shepherdess, but she scorns him; Rosalind/Ganymede rebukes her for her unkindness, whereupon Phebe falls in love with her. Touchstone woos a country girl, Audrey, and discomfits her rustic lover.

Oliver arrives in the forest, looking for Orlando. Orlando saves him from a lioness, and is wounded in doing so. This brings about a change of heart in Oliver, who repents of his previous evil deeds and is reconciled to Orlando. Oliver and Celia fall in love at first sight, and agree to get married. Rosalind and Celia assemble all the prospective couples, and reveal their true identity. The Duke agrees that Rosalind shall marry Orlando; Phebe agrees to marry Silvius; Oliver is to marry Celia; and Touchstone is to marry Audrey. Another brother of Orlando and Oliver arrives to report that Duke Frederick had mounted a military expedition against the exiles in the Forest of Arden; at the edge of the forest, however, he had met an old religious man and undergone a religious conversion; he had renounced the world, given the dukedom back to his brother, and restored the lands of those who were in exile with him. There is general festivity. In an epilogue, Rosalind asks for the audience's indulgence for the play.

Detailed summaries

Act I Scene 1

From a conversation between Orlando and Adam, we learn that Orlando had been left a mere thousand crowns in his father's will, and that his eldest brother, Oliver, is now denying him education and keeping him at home unoccupied and treated like a menial. Oliver enters, and Orlando quarrels with him, demanding either to be brought up in the way befitting a gentleman, or to be given his thousand crowns with which to seek his fortune elsewhere. In a soliloquy, Oliver reveals that he has no intention of giving Orlando his thousand crowns, and that he is plotting something against him. Oliver is visited by Charles, Duke Frederick's wrestler, and we learn of the situation at court: Duke Frederick has seized power from his elder brother, Duke Senior, and banished him; Duke Senior is in the Forest of Arden with a number of lords who are faithful to him, and is every day joined by more gentlemen; his daughter Rosalind, however, has been permitted to stay at court, because of the love felt for her by Duke Frederick's daughter. Charles tells Oliver that Orlando intends to be one of the challengers who wrestles with him before the Duke the following day; he fears that Orlando may be hurt, and asks Oliver to dissuade him from taking part. Oliver replies that Orlando is stubborn, and will not be dissuaded; moreover, he is villainous and vindictive, and if Charles defeats him he will plot against his life. Charles believes Oliver, and goes away determined to disable Orlando in the wrestling.

NOTES AND GLOSSARY:

Remember that many commonly-occurring words are glossed on page 19 in Part 1 above.

bequeathed: the subject *he* (Orlando's father) must be understood before *bequeathed*, and is also the subject of *charged* ('instructed'). In F1 a colon has probably dropped out after *fashion*

fair with their feeding: of fine appearance because of the way they are fed

manage: the action and paces to which a horse is trained in the riding-school

hinds: servants, farm labourers

mines my gentility: undermines my status as a gentleman

what make you here?: what are you doing here? But Orlando in his reply uses *make* in the sense 'create, produce, fashion'

be naught: efface yourself, withdraw, be quiet

keep your hogs . . . prodigal portion: a reference to the biblical story of the Prodigal Son (Luke 15.11–32). The younger of two sons asked his father for his share of the inheritance; on receiving it, he went to a distant country and spent it all on riotous living. Then there was a famine, and the Prodigal Son took service with a man of that country and was sent into his fields to feed his hogs; and he was so hungry that he ate the husks that the hogs were fed on. (The remainder of the story tells of the Prodigal's return home, and how he was received by his father and his brother)

in the gentle condition . . . know me: you should recognise that I have the standing of a gentleman by birth

courtesy of nations: usage of civilised nations

you are too young in this: you are inexperienced in this [physical combat]. Oliver strikes or attacks Orlando, who retaliates by seizing him by the throat

exercises: employment, education

grow upon me: take liberties with me; grow up (and so become troublesome to me)

physic your rankness: cure (purge) your insolence (over-rapid growth)
Robin Hood: a legendary English outlaw of the Middle Ages, whose daring feats were the subject of many ballads and tales. He lived with his followers in Sherwood Forest, near Nottingham, and was noted for his chivalry, his skill as a bowman, and his championing of the poor and oppressed against the rich and unscrupulous
the golden world: in classical mythology, the Golden Age was an ideal period in the remote past, when men lived in complete peace and justice, in harmony with nature, and without having to labour
underhand: unobtrusive, quiet
I had as lief: I would be just as glad if
practise: plot, lay evil schemes
indirect: devious, deceitful, unjust
if ever he go alone: if ever he is able to walk unaided
gamester: athlete
kindle the boy thither: incite Orlando to go there

Act I Scene 2

Celia, Duke Frederick's daughter, comforts her cousin Rosalind, daughter of the banished duke: when her father dies, Celia will return the dukedom to Rosalind. Touchstone, the court jester, comes to summon Celia to her father; they exchange pleasantries. A courtier, Le Beau, brings the news that the wrestler, Charles, has thrown and fatally injured three young brothers; the wrestling is to continue at the place where they now are. Duke Frederick and his followers enter, with Charles and Orlando. The Duke asks Rosalind and Celia to dissuade Orlando from wrestling; they speak to him, but he persists in his resolve. Orlando and Charles wrestle; Charles is defeated and is carried off. The Duke asks Orlando his name, and is displeased to learn that he is the son of a former enemy; he goes off without rewarding Orlando. Rosalind and Celia are shocked at the Duke's treatment of Orlando, and stay behind to thank and encourage him; Rosalind gives Orlando a chain, and he is so overcome by emotion that he is unable even to thank her. Le Beau returns to warn Orlando to leave at once, since the Duke is displeased with him. Orlando recognises that Rosalind has won his heart.

NOTES AND GLOSSARY:

so thou hadst been: provided that you had been
righteously tempered: made of the right ingredients
render . . . affection: return to you out of love

come off again: retreat, extricate yourself (punning on the military and sexual meanings of *honour*)

housewife Fortune . . . wheel: Fortune (the Roman goddess Fortuna) was a common theme in Renaissance literature and art. She was depicted as a female figure, turning a wheel on which men rise and fall, or balancing blindfold on a rolling stone. By calling Fortune a housewife, Celia humorously turns her wheel into a spinning-wheel

fair . . . honest . . . ill-favouredly: beautiful . . . chaste . . . ugly

Fortune . . . Nature: Fortune gives men such things as wealth and power, but beauty and ugliness are the gifts of Nature

natural: an idiot, half-witted person

by mine honour: an expression appropriate only to people of high rank, since only the gentry could claim to have honour. This is why Rosalind questions Touchstone's use of the phrase

stand to it: avouch, insist

put on us: force on us

colour: kind, character

keep . . . my rank: maintain my high status (by using suitably pompous language). In her interruption, Rosalind puns on another meaning of *rank*, 'evil-smelling'

bills on their necks: (a) spears over their shoulders, (b) notices hung round their necks

Be it known . . . presents: a standard opening in many official documents and proclamations, *these presents* meaning 'this present document'. Rosalind is punning on *presence*

dole: lamentation, expression of sorrow

broken music: part music, music arranged for different instruments

Flourish: a fanfare on brass instruments, used to signal the approach of a person of high rank

there is such odds in the man: the man (Charles) has such superiority

Hercules be thy speed: may Hercules make you successful. In classical mythology, Hercules (the Latin name for Herakles) was a Greek hero, son of the king of the gods (Zeus) and a mortal woman. He was enormously strong, and when he fought the Nemean lion, the skin of which was invulnerable to all weapons, he killed it be wrestling with it and strangling it

If I had a thunderbolt . . . down: if Celia were able to hurl a thunderbolt simply by looking at an opponent, she would use it against Charles

Sticks me at heart: pierces me to the heart, deeply grieves me
out of suits: out of favour
quintain: a solid post or plank set up as a mark for lancers to tilt at, or as a target for darts or arrows
My pride fell with my fortunes: Rosalind is offering an excuse for her conduct. She has been going away slowly, hoping for Orlando to say something to call her back; but Orlando is so overcome that he is unable to speak. Rosalind, however, is so much attracted to him that she pretends he has called them back, and gives him another chance to speak to her. She knows that this is rather forward conduct, unbefitting a princess, and offers her excuse accordingly
she urged conference: she pressed me to talk to her
misconsters: misconstrues. Stressed on the second syllable
from the smoke . . . smother: a proverbial expression, meaning 'from a bad situation to an even worse one'; *smother* was dense, suffocating smoke

Act I Scene 3

Rosalind admits to Celia that she has fallen in love with Orlando. The Duke accuses Rosalind of treason, and banishes her from his court on pain of death; he rejects both Rosalind's defence of herself and Celia's pleas for her. Celia tells Rosalind that she will accompany her in her exile; they will go to look for Rosalind's father in the Forest of Arden. They agree to disguise themselves, Celia as a girl of humble rank, and Rosalind as a young man. They will persuade Touchstone, the court jester, to accompany them.

NOTES AND GLOSSARY:

Cupid: the Roman god of love
burs: (a) the prickly heads of certain common plants, which stick to a rough surface; they are often thrown at people in sport by children, so that they stick to their clothes; (b) something that appears to stick in the throat, causing huskiness, and needing to be cleared by coughing
Hem: cough
you will try in time: in due course you will have a wrestling match (with Orlando)
chase: sequence of arguments
dearly: deeply, strongly, grievously
with your safest haste: as quickly as possible, for your own safety

intelligence: communication, intercourse
ranged along: gone off roaming, become a vagabond
Juno's swans: in Roman mythology, Juno was the principal goddess, wife of Jupiter. It was, however, the chariot of Venus (goddess of love) which was drawn by swans, not that of Juno
umber: a kind of brown earth used as a pigment. Aristocratic ladies were careful to preserve their fair complexions, whereas the faces of peasant-girls were darkened by exposure to the sun and weather, so Celia needs to darken her face as part of her disguise
curtle-axe short broad cutting-sword, cutlass
swashing: swaggering, dashing
outface . . . semblances: brazen things out by means of their outward appearance
Jove's own page . . . Ganymede: in Roman mythology, Jove (or Jupiter) was king of the gods; Ganymede was his cup-bearer
Aliena: a Latin word meaning 'foreign woman, woman belonging to another place'

Act II Scene 1

In the Forest of Arden, Duke Senior and his followers congratulate themselves on the delights of country life, compared with life at court. One of the lords describes to the Duke how he has overheard the melancholy Jaques moralising on the death of a deer.

NOTES AND GLOSSARY:

the penalty of Adam: it was believed that, when Adam and Eve were in the Garden of Eden, there were no seasons: it was perpetual spring. The seasons were one of the consequences of the Fall
feelingly: by making themselves felt
toad . . . venomous . . . jewel: the toad was believed to be poisonous, and to have in its head a jewel (a toadstone) which was of great medicinal value
exempt from public haunt: removed from places of common resort
fools: simpletons. Here used as a term of endearment rather than of contempt (and similarly in line 40)
confines: region, territory. Stressed on the second syllable
forked heads: the barbed heads of arrows
Jaques: pronounced as two syllables
antick: fantastically shaped; ancient

sequestered: separated (from the herd)
moralize: make the subject of moral reflection, interpret morally
needless: not in need (of more water)
of his velvet friend: by his smooth-coated kinsman. *Velvet* refers to the smoothness and softness of the deer's skin
misery doth part The flux of company: the miserable person goes away from other people, who are like a flood or flowing stream (*flux*)
most invectively: with bitterest denunciation
kill . . . up: massacre, exterminate
cope: meet, encounter

Act II Scene 2

Duke Frederick questions his courtiers about the disappearance of Celia and Rosalind. It is suspected that Orlando may be with them. The Duke orders Oliver to be brought before him.

NOTES AND GLOSSARY:
Are of consent . . . this: have consented to this and permitted it
untreasured of: with its treasure (Celia) missing
roynish: scurvy, base
Send to . . . brother to me: the messengers are to go to Oliver's house, and fetch Orlando (*that gallant*) to the Duke. If Orlando is not there, they are to fetch Oliver, and the Duke will make him find Orlando
inquisition quail: investigation slacken

Act II Scene 3

Orlando, returning to Oliver's house after the wrestling, is warned by Adam not to come in, since Oliver is plotting to murder him. Orlando does not know what to do. Adam offers him the five hundred crowns which he had saved from his wages under Orlando's father, and says he will accompany him as his servant. They go off together to seek their livelihood elsewhere.

NOTES AND GLOSSARY:
what make you here?: what are you doing here?
bonny: large, powerful
prizer: one who engages in contest for reward (Charles the wrestler)
use to lie: are in the habit of sleeping
practices: schemes, plots, intrigues

This is no place . . . butchery: this is not a dwelling-house but a slaughter-house
diverted blood: blood diverted from the course of nature (unnatural behaviour of a brother)
The thrifty hire I saved: the wages which I thriftily saved
He . . . ravens . . . sparrow: God. The Bible refers to God's providence in providing for birds, and specifically for ravens and sparrows
with unbashful forehead: brazenly, shamelessly
In lieu of: in return for, as a reward for
come thy ways: come along
too late a week: far too late

Act II Scene 4

Rosalind, Celia, and Touchstone arrive exhausted in the Forest of Arden. They overhear a conversation between Corin (an old shepherd) and Silvius (a young one) about love, in which Silvius expresses his passion for Phebe (a shepherdess). This gives occasion for sighing by Rosalind and parody by Touchstone. They ask Corin where they can find food and shelter. He tells them that the sheep-farm where he works is being sold; they say that they would like to buy it, and go off with him to inspect it.

NOTES AND GLOSSARY:
Jupiter: the king of the gods in Roman mythology
weaker vessel: woman. A biblical expression
doublet-and-hose: normal man's clothes in Shakespeare's time. The doublet was a close-fitting jacket, and hose were breeches
bear no cross: (a) undergo no affliction (with a reference to the cross of Christ); (b) carry no money (many coins had the figure of a cross on one side)
searching of: examining with a probe (surgical instrument)
hard adventure: cruel accident (chance)
bid him take that: 'him' refers to Touchstone's imaginary rival, and 'that' is a blow
batler: wooden bat for beating clothes during laundering
chopt: chapped
peascod: pea-pod. But perhaps Touchstone means the whole pea-plant, the two *cods* being pea-pods (probably with a pun on *cods* 'testicles')
as all is mortal . . . mortal in folly: just as everything in nature is certain to die, so is anybody in love certain to be extremely foolish

ware of: (a) conscious of, (b) careful in avoiding, on my guard against
Jove: another name for Jupiter (see note above)
clown: (a) rustic, peasant; (b) fool, jester, idiot
entertainment: hospitality
recks: cares, wishes
bounds of feed: the tract of land within which he has the right to graze his sheep
swain: shepherd (Silvius)
stand with: is consistent with
to pay for it of us: something from us to pay for it with. Before they fled from court, Celia and Rosalind planned to take their money and jewels with them (I.3.132), and obviously did so (despite Touchstone's joke in line 11 about Celia's lack of money)
feeder: servant, dependent

Act II Scene 5

Amiens, one of the exiled lords, sings a pastoral song to Jaques and other followers of Duke Senior. Jaques parodies it.

NOTES AND GLOSSARY:

turn: shape, form, fashion
Unto . . . throat: so that it resembles the sweet song of a bird
ragged: rough, harsh
stanzo: a common sixteenth-century variant of *stanza*
dog-apes: baboons
renders me the beggarly thanks: in return gives me thanks, which befit a beggar
cover the while: meanwhile lay the table
look you: look for you
disputable: disputatious, argumentative
live i'th'sun: live outdoors
to this note: to be sung to this tune
in despite of my invention: as a mark of scorn for my own creative powers. In rhetorical theory, *invention* was the first stage of the creative process, in which suitable material was found for the oration or literary work
pass . . . ass: an exact rhyme in Shakespeare's day, both words having short /a/
Ducdame: Jaques is deliberately teasing his audience with an incomprehensible word. It must be pronounced as three syllables

the first-born of Egypt: a biblical reference. On the night when the Israelites fled from their captivity in Egypt, God killed the eldest child in every Egyptian family (Exodus 12.29–30)
banquet: a light meal, especially of sweetmeats, fruit, and wine

Act II Scene 6

Orlando and Adam have arrived in the Forest of Arden. Adam is exhausted, and weak from lack of food. Orlando encourages him, and says he will carry him to a place of shelter and then find him some food.

NOTES AND GLOSSARY:
uncouth: desolate, wild
conceit: imagination
comfortable: cheerful
Well said: well done
desert: wild, uncultivated region

Act II Scene 7

With great glee, Jaques tells Duke Senior and his followers that he has met a fool in the forest (Touchstone). He wishes that he could himself be a licensed jester, and defends his satirical habits against the Duke's criticism. Orlando bursts in and threatens to kill them unless they give him food. To his surprise, the Duke answers civilly and invites him to join them at table. He apologises for his rudeness, and goes off to fetch Adam. Jaques moralises on the life of man, which is like a stage-play with seven acts (seven stages in a man's life). Orlando returns with Adam, and they are given food. The Duke learns who Orlando is, and welcomes him.

NOTES AND GLOSSARY:
compact of jars: composed of discords
discord in the spheres: it was inconceivable that there could be discord in the spheres, so the Duke is expressing disbelief in Jaques's alleged musicality. On the Music of the Spheres, see p. 8 in Part 1 above
motley: a woollen cloth of mixed colour. Fools and professional jesters wore as their distinctive uniform a long coat or gown made of motley
Lady Fortune: see note on 'housewife Fortune' (I.2.30) above
dial from his poke: timepiece (watch or portable sundial) from his bag
moral: moralise

Chanticleer: a cock. Chanticleer was the name usually given to the cock in medieval beast-fables
sans intermission: without stopping
brain . . . dry: a dry brain was thought to have a good memory
remainder biscuit: ship's biscuits left over
vents: utters
suit: (a) request, (b) set of clothes
bob: blow; taunt, bitter jest
squandering glances: widely scattered satirical hits
counter: token (as opposed to a real coin), something worthless
brutish sting: sexual desire, lust
embossed: swollen
headed: having come to a head (like a boil)
says his bravery . . . cost: says that his splendid clothes are not paid for by me (and that I therefore have no right to criticise him for them)
free: innocent
You touched my vein at first: your first suggestion correctly diagnosed my state of mind
inland bred: brought up near the metropolis, not provincial
upon command: simply by asking for it
modern instances: commonplace examples
pantaloon: feeble and foolish old man. Pantaloon was one of the stock characters of Italian comedy
well saved: carefully preserved, kept in good condition
wind . . . unkind: an exact rhyme. The present-day pronunciation of *wind* is descended from an originally non-standard variant
warp: distort, change the shape of, blow about. The word rhymed exactly with *sharp*, both words having short /a/, and the /r/ being pronounced
effigies: likeness, portrait, image. Stressed on the second syllable
limned: painted

Act III Scene 1

Duke Frederick questions Oliver about Orlando's disappearance. He orders him to bring Orlando back, dead or alive, within a year. Meanwhile, he seizes all of Oliver's property.

NOTES AND GLOSSARY:
argument: object

Seek him with candle: look for him diligently
turn: return
quit thee: prove yourself innocent
extent: seizure in execution of a writ
expediently: quickly, promptly
turn him going: send him on his way

Act III Scene 2

Orlando hangs verses in praise of Rosalind on trees in the forest. Corin and Touchstone debate the merits of court life and country life. Rosalind enters reading one of Orlando's poems; Touchstone parodies it. Celia enters reading another; she reveals to Rosalind that Orlando is in the forest and that the poems are his. Orlando and Jaques enter, and engage in a wit-combat about love. Rosalind (still in disguise) accosts Orlando; after a discussion about time, they talk about love, which Rosalind attacks as a form of lunacy. She offers to cure Orlando of his love: he is to pretend that she is Rosalind, and woo her under that name; in response, she will behave in a coquettish and capricious fashion, and thus drive his love out. Orlando does not wish to be cured of love, but he does wish to talk about Rosalind, and he agrees to undergo the treatment.

NOTES AND GLOSSARY:

thrice-crowned . . . night: the moon. In classical mythology, the moon-goddess had three different forms and names – Greek Artemis (on earth), Persephone (in the underworld), and Selene (in heaven), or Latin Diana, Proserpina, and Luna. She was also often identified with the goddess Hecate. One of the characteristics of Artemis/Diana was chastity
Thy huntress: Rosalind. Artemis/Diana carried a bow and was a huntress. She was followed by a band of nymphs, also chaste and huntresses. Orlando is saying that Rosalind is one of these nymphs
character: engrave, write
unexpressive she: indescribable woman
spare: frugal, abstemious
stomach: inclination
complain of good breeding: complain that he has not been well brought up
a natural philosopher: (a) a scientist, (b) a philosopher who is a fool
manners: Touchstone's argument depends on a pun on *manners*: (a) polite behaviour, (b) morals

parlous: perilous
Instance: give an example
fells: coats, fleeces
worm's meat: food for worms
in respect of: compared to
perpend: consider
flux: discharge, substance discharged. Civet is a perfume obtained from a gland in the anal pouch of the civet-cat
raw: (a) inexperienced, uncultivated, (b) uncooked. One way of cooking meat was to score it with a knife (*make incision*) before grilling it. The idea of grilling arises from the suggestion that Corin is damned (will go to Hell)
get: earn
bell-wether: the leading sheep in a flock, which had a bell attached to its neck
cuckoldy: an old ram would have large horns, and horns were the emblem of a cuckold
Ind . . . Rosalind: all the rhymes in this poem were exact ones. Touchstone's criticism of it is not that the rhymes are imperfect, but that it keeps on monotonously with the same rhyme and has a jog-trot rhythm
Ind: Indies
fairest lined: most beautifully drawn
right butter-women's . . . market: just like a series of women carrying their butter to market. A comment on the monotonous rhymes and uncouth rhythms of the poem
after kind: (behave) according to its nature
lined: (a) provided with a lining (for warmth), (b) mated, subjected to sexual intercourse. In the sexual sense, the word was used of dogs and wolves
to cart: carts were used for carrying away the corn after harvest, but also for the punishment of prostitutes, who were whipped and publicly displayed in a cart
prick: (a) thorn (of the rose), (b) male sexual organ. Touchstone's poem is full of indecent puns
false gallop: canter
graff: graft
medlar: the fruit of the medlar-tree, resembling a small apple. It was not eaten until soft and pulpy in the middle (*rotten*). With a pun on *meddler*
civil: civilised

span: the distance from the tip of the thumb to the tip of the little finger. Such a small distance encloses (*buckles in*) the whole of a man's life (*his sum of age*). This echoes the Bible (Psalms 39.5)

in little: in miniature, in a small space

Helen's cheek: the beauty of Helen of Troy. Helen was the wife of Menelaus, King of Sparta; her abduction by Paris, son of the King of Troy, was the cause of the Trojan War

Cleopatra: a queen of Egypt (69–30BC), notorious for her seductiveness

Atalanta: in Greek mythology, the daughter of Iasus of Calydon. She was the fastest runner of her time, and to avoid marriage she made it a condition that any suitor should race against her, and be killed if he lost. Her better part was presumably her chastity, and her worse part her cruelty to her suitors

Lucretia: the wife of Collatinus, a Roman nobleman of the sixth century BC. She was raped by Sextus, son of the last King of Rome, and committed suicide to demonstrate her faithfulness to her husband. The episode triggered off the revolt against the Tarquin kings which led to their expulsion and the establishment of the Roman Republic

have . . . slave: an exact rhyme, depending on the old stressed form of *have* (still heard in the compound *behave*)

bag and baggage: the total property of an army. To retreat with bag and baggage was to make an honourable retreat, without losing anything

scrip and scrippage: a scrip was a shepherd's wallet; *scrippage* is Touchstone's jocular coinage to parallel *baggage*

nine days: a nine days' wonder is something that creates a sensation for a short time

Pythagoras: an ancient Greek philosopher, who held the doctrine of the transmigration of souls: after a man's death, his soul is reincarnated in another body, which may be that of an animal

Irish rat: there was a belief in Ireland that rats could be killed by the recitation of suitable poems

Trow: believe

out of all whooping: beyond what can be expressed by cries of excitement

One inch . . . South Sea of discovery: the least further delay will seem as long as a voyage of exploration to the South Seas

sad brow: with a serious expression on your face

Gargantua: a large-mouthed giant in a series of books by the sixteenth-century French humorist François Rabelais
Wherein went he?: how was he dressed?
Jove's tree: in Roman mythology, the oak tree was sacred to Jove (Jupiter)
holla: an exclamation meaning 'Stop!'.
heart: with a pun on *hart* 'deer'
burden: refrain or chorus to a song, or bass accompaniment to it. Here referring to Rosalind's constant interruptions of Celia's story
moe: more
ill-favouredly: badly
just: exactly so, just so
conned: learned, committed to memory
out of rings: it was common for finger-rings to have short mottoes (posies) inscribed on them
painted cloth: cheap wall-hanging adorned with pictures, often of moral or biblical subjects, and often also with mottoes
Atalanta: see note on Atalanta (line 143) above
cipher: figure nought, nothing
trots hard: goes at an uncomfortable trot
se'nnight: week
ambles: moves smoothly and easily. The amble was a pace in which the horse lifted the two feet on one side together, alternately with the two feet on the other
lean and wasteful learning: study which makes a man thin and causes him to waste away
cony: rabbit
kindled: born
purchase: acquire
removed: remote
religious: belonging to a religious order
courtship: (a) courtliness, behaviour appropriate at court, (b) wooing
fancy-monger: trader in love (contemptuous)
quotidian: a quotidian fever (one which recurs every day)
blue eye: eye with dark rings round it
unquestionable: not submitting to interrogation, impatient
point-device: perfectly correct or neat
dark house and a whip: a common treatment for the insane
moonish: changeable, fickle
wash your liver: the liver was believed to be the seat of the passions

Act III Scene 3

Touchstone converses with Audrey, a country girl, while Jaques watches unseen. By Touchstone's arrangement, a local vicar, Martext, arrives to marry them. Jaques interrupts, and tells Touchstone to get married properly in church. Touchstone and Audrey go away with him, leaving an indignant Martext.

NOTES AND GLOSSARY:

Ovid . . . Goths: the Latin poet Ovid (43BC–AD18) was in later life banished by the Emperor Augustus to Tomis on the Black Sea. The Goths were a Germanic people from the Baltic area who later penetrated to many parts of southern and eastern Europe; they did not, however, settle in the Black Sea area until the third century of our era. Touchstone's pun (*goats/Goths*) depends on a variant of *Goth* with a long vowel. There is also a learned pun in *capricious*, which is derived from the Latin word for a goat

ill-inhabited: lodged in an unsuitable dwelling (Touchstone)

Jove in a thatched house: a reference to the story (told by Ovid in his *Metamorphoses*) in which the gods Jupiter (Jove) and Mercury visited Phrygia in disguise. The only people that welcomed them and gave them hospitality were a poverty-stricken old couple called Philemon and Baucis, who lived (Ovid says) in a humble cottage with a roof made of thatch and reeds

seconded of: supported by, encouraged by

great reckoning . . . room: a large bill for meagre accommodation. There may also be a reference to the death of the dramatist Christopher Marlowe, who in 1593 was killed in a quarrel about the bill in a private room in a tavern

hard-favoured: ugly

material: unspiritual, worldly

foul: (a) ugly, (b) morally corrupt

Sir Oliver Martext: perhaps a puritan, since *Martext* ('spoil text') is modelled on *Marprelate*, the pseudonym of a group of puritan pamphleteers of 1588–9. The title *Sir* was commonly given to a priest

stagger: hesitate, waver

horn-beasts: animals with horns, such as sheep and deer. They would daunt a man bent on marriage because horns were the emblem of the cuckold

rascal: a young, lean, or inferior deer
toy: trifle, something unimportant
pray be covered: please put your hat on. A man removed his hat in the presence of a social superior, who could then as a sign of affability tell him to put it on again. Touchstone is pretending that Jaques has taken off his hat in deference to his higher rank
bow: yoke
green timber: unseasoned timber, which shrinks with age

Act III Scene 4

Rosalind and Celia discuss Orlando. Corin tells them that Silvius is engaged in an unsuccessful wooing of Phebe, and undertakes to place them where they can observe it.

NOTES AND GLOSSARY:

browner than Judas's: Judas Iscariot was the follower of Christ who betrayed him to his enemies (Matthew 26.14–16, 47–50). In Christian art he was traditionally depicted with red hair
his kisses . . . Judas's own children: his kisses are insincere, those of a betrayer. Judas betrayed Christ by kissing him, to indicate to his enemies which man they were to arrest
holy bread: bread which was blessed by the priest and distributed to the congregation after the service of Holy Communion
cast: this may be an example of the very rare word *cast* meaning 'chaste', from Latin *castus*. More probably, however, it means 'cast off, discarded': Celia suggests jocularly that Orlando has bought a pair of old second-hand lips from Diana, the Roman goddess who was patroness of virginity (see notes on Diana on p. 36)
concave: hollow
brave: splendid
traverse: obliquely. Orlando breaks his oath on his lady's heart, just as an unskilful jouster (*puisny tilter*) breaks his lance by striking the target obliquely instead of straight
pageant: scene acted on the stage, show
remove . . . love: a rhyme. There was a variant pronunciation of *love* with a long /u:/

Act III Scene 5

Rosalind, Celia, and Corin watch unobserved while Silvius pleads for Phebe's love and she rejects him. Rosalind comes forward and rebukes Phebe for being proud and pitiless. Phebe promptly falls in love with Rosalind (Ganymede). When she is alone with Silvius again, she can talk of nothing but Rosalind; she asks Silvius to carry a letter to 'him', pretending that it is a hostile and taunting one.

NOTES AND GLOSSARY:

coward gates: eyelids

cicatrice and capable impressure: mark and impression received

ordinary of nature's sale-work: commonplace line of nature's ready-made goods

bugle: (resembling a) black glass bead

entame: subdue, make tame

south: south wind

Cry the man mercy: beg the man's pardon

Dead Shepherd: the poet and dramatist Christopher Marlowe (1564–93); the *saw* (saying, maxim) that Phebe quotes is taken from his poem *Hero and Leander*

extermined: ended, destroyed

carlot: churl, peasant

damask: material made from silk, often of several colours

In parcels: in detail, point by point

am remembered: remember, recall

Omittance is no quittance: failure to pay a debt does not absolve one from it

Act IV Scene 1

Rosalind and Jaques discuss melancholy. Orlando woos the disguised Rosalind as arranged. He goes away to keep an appointment, and promises to return in two hours. Rosalind expresses to Celia the depth of her love for him.

NOTES AND GLOSSARY:

simples: ingredients

Cupid hath clapped him o'th'shoulder: Cupid (the god of love) has arrested him (but he is not yet in prison)

leer: face, appearance

gravelled: stuck (like a ship which has run aground)

Who could be out: Orlando means 'Who could be at a loss (for words)?', but Rosalind puns, taking *out* to mean 'not engaged in sexual intercourse'

Troilus: a famous lover of romance. He was a son of the King of Troy during the Trojan War, and loved Cressida, who was unfaithful to him. He was killed in battle by the Greek hero Achilles

Leander: a poem called *Hero and Leander*, begun by Christopher Marlowe and completed by George Chapman, was published in 1598. Hero was a priestess at Sestos. Leander, her lover, lived at Abydos on the other side of the Hellespont. To visit her, Leander swam across the Hellespont each night, but on one of these journeys he was drowned. Rosalind's account is a light-hearted parody

your commission: what authority you have (for taking me)

goes before the priest: (a) anticipates the priest (she says she will marry Orlando before the priest has asked her), (b) appears before the priest (to be married)

Barbary cock-pigeon: a fancy variety of pigeon originally introduced from Barbary (North Africa). The cock-pigeon was traditionally believed to be extremely jealous

against rain: when rain is imminent

Diana in the fountain: a statue of the goddess Diana was often the centrepiece of a fountain. There is perhaps also a reference to the central character of Montemeyer's famous pastoral romance *Diana* (1559)

hyen: hyena

Make the doors: shut the door

Wit, whither wilt?: wit, where are you off to? A proverbial expression directed at a chatterer

check: reproof, rebuke

her husband's occasion: an opportunity to put her husband in the wrong

misused: abused, slandered

Bay of Portugal: the sea off the west coast of Portugal is very deep: fifty miles from Lisbon, it is more than four thousand metres. This is a greater depth than sailors in Shakespeare's time were able to sound

bastard of Venus . . . blind rascally boy: Cupid, the Roman god of love, son of Venus, the goddess of love. He was depicted as a blind child with a bow and arrows

shadow: place in the shade

Act IV Scene 2

Some of Duke Senior's followers have killed a deer. They sing a triumphant song.

NOTES AND GLOSSARY:

deer's horns upon his head: with the usual joke (the horns would be a sign that the man was a cuckold)

Act IV Scene 3

Rosalind and Celia are waiting for Orlando, who is late. Silvius brings Rosalind the letter from Phebe; he believes it is an insulting one, and apologises. Rosalind pretends that it is, and accuses Silvius of having written it himself. She then reads it to him, and it proves to be a love-letter. She reproaches Silvius for loving such a woman as Phebe, and sends him back to her. Oliver arrives, looking for Rosalind and Celia. He recounts how Orlando had found him sleeping in the wood, and had rescued him from a lioness; as a result of this act, Oliver had undergone a change of heart and been reconciled to his brother. In the fight with the lioness, Orlando had been wounded, and now sends Oliver to apologise to them for his failure to keep his appointment, and to give a bloody handkerchief to the youth he calls his Rosalind. Rosalind faints; when they bring her round she pretends she has been play-acting, but she is so weak that they have to help her back to the cottage.

NOTES AND GLOSSARY:

Bear this, bear all: if I could put up with this, I could put up with anything

phoenix: a mythical bird, the only one of its kind, which lived in the Arabian desert. Every five hundred years it burnt itself to ashes, from which it then emerged with renewed youth

turned into the extremity: brought into the most extreme degree

freestone: fine-grained sandstone or limestone

Turk to Christian: in the sixteenth century the Ottoman Turks ruled a large empire, including Egypt and what are now Greece, Hungary, Yugoslavia, Albania, Bulgaria, and Rumania. There was frequent war between the Turks and their Christian neighbours to the west

Ethiop: negro, black. The letter is written in black ink, and is even blacker (more malignant) in its purport (*effect*)

She Phebes me: she behaves to me in a manner typical of Phebe (cruelly, tyrannically)

Meaning me a beast: Phebe says that the eye of man has not been able to have any effect (*vengeance*) on her; Rosalind jocularly interprets this to mean that she herself (whose eye has certainly affected Phebe) is an animal. In fact Phebe means that she is a god

eyne: eyes. An archaic plural even in Shakespeare's day
love . . . move: an exact rhyme (see note on *remove*, III.4.51-2, above)
by him seal up your mind: using Silvius as a messenger, send me a sealed letter telling me your decision
youth and kind: youthful nature
purlieus: tracts of land on the edge of a forest
neighbour bottom: nearby valley
rank of osiers: row of willow-trees
bestows himself: behaves, has the demeanour of
indented: undulating, zigzag
royal disposition of that beast . . . dead: it was commonly believed that a lion would not eat carrion. The lion is *royal* because it is the king of beasts
hurtling: conflict
recountments: stories, narrations
Heigh-ho: an exclamation expressing weariness, resignation, or sighing

Act V Scene 1

Touchstone assures Audrey that they will get married. William, a local youth who has an interest in Audrey, is interrogated by Touchstone, threatened by him, and dismissed.

NOTES AND GLOSSARY:

find a time: to get married
the old gentleman: Jaques
Cover thy head: see note on *pray be covered* in III.3
ipse: Latin pronoun meaning 'he himself, the chief person'. Here used to mean 'the successful suitor'
bastinado: beating with a stick, cudgelling
God rest: may God keep

Act V Scene 2

Oliver tells Orlando that he and Aliena (Celia) have fallen in love, and intend to get married; Oliver will give his inheritance to Orlando and remain in the forest as a shepherd. Rosalind tells Orlando that she has skill in magic arts: if he really loves Rosalind, she will set her before him the following day and he will be able to marry her. Phebe reproaches Rosalind for having shown her letter to Silvius. Silvius, Phebe, Orlando, and Rosalind perform a set piece on the nature of love. Rosalind tells them all to meet on the following day, and they will have their desires fulfilled.

NOTES AND GLOSSARY:

all's: all his

swound: swoon, faint

I know where you are: I know what you are talking about

thrasonical: boastful. Thraso is a boastful soldier in Terence's play *The Eunuch*

Caesar's thrasonical brag . . . overcame: Julius Caesar (c. 101–44 BC), the celebrated Roman soldier and statesman, used this famous expression (Veni, vidi, vici) in a letter to a friend in Rome, to describe how he defeated an army led by Pharnaces in Asia Minor in 47 BC

degrees: steps. With a reference to the rhetorical figure, *gradatio* or *climax*, which Rosalind has just used (see p. 73). The literal meaning of Latin *gradatio* is 'series of steps, staircase'

pair of stairs: flight of stairs

incontinent: (a) immediately, without delay, (b) unchaste

clubs cannot part them: clubs (heavy sticks) were the weapons carried by London apprentices, and would be used to separate the combatants in a brawl

conceit: understanding, intelligence

magician . . . art . . . not damnable: the practice of black magic, which involved collaboration with the Devil, was damnable (that is, was a sin which would cause the practitioner to be damned, to go to Hell); but some people believed that it was also possible to use white magic, which involved no recourse to the powers of evil, and which was not sinful provided it was used only for good ends

gesture cries out: behaviour proclaims

inconvenient: morally wrong, improper

human as she is: in flesh and blood, in her own person (not as a mere phantom)

tender dearly: value highly. The practice of witchcraft was illegal, and in some cases could be punished by death

despiteful: contemptuous, malicious, insulting

observance: respectful attention, dutiful service

Why do you speak too: in view of Orlando's reply, many editors emend to 'Who do you speak to'

howling . . . Irish wolves . . . moon: it was believed that dogs and wolves were especially likely to howl continuously at the time of the full moon. By Shakespeare's time, wolves had been virtually exterminated in England, but they were still very common in Ireland

Act V Scene 3

Touchstone and Audrey are to be married the following day. Two pages sing them a song.

NOTES AND GLOSSARY:

woman of the world: married woman
clap into't roundly: go straight into it briskly
hawking: clearing the throat noisily, coughing
on a horse: on one horse. So *in a tune* means 'singing one (the same) tune'; this could mean either that the boys sang in unison, or that they sang in canon
With a hey . . . nonino: a meaningless refrain, as also is 'hey, ding a ding, ding'
lass . . . pass: an exact rhyme in Shakespeare's time, both words being pronounced with short /a/
ring time: time when lovers exchange rings
acres: in the old open-field system of cultivation, an acre was the area of each cultivated strip in the field, the strips being separated by balks (low ridges of earth)
the prime: (a) the spring, (b) the springtime of human life, youth
matter in the ditty: substance in the words of the song
note . . . untuneable: the music was extremely unmelodious. Touchstone's joke is that he says *untunable* when the structure of the sentence leads us to expect *tunable*

Act V Scene 4

In the presence of Duke Senior and his courtiers, Rosalind reiterates the agreement that has been entered into: if Rosalind appears, the Duke agrees that he will give her in marriage to Orlando, and Orlando agrees that he will marry her; Phebe agrees that she will marry Ganymede (Rosalind), or, if she changes her mind, that she will instead marry Silvius; Silvius agrees that in that event he will marry Phebe. Rosalind and Celia go off. Touchstone and Audrey enter, and Touchstone entertains the company with a discourse on quarrelling. Rosalind and Celia return dressed in their own clothes, accompanied by somebody representing Hymen, who pronounces a solemn blessing on the couples. All puzzles are now resolved, and the four couples are agreed on marriage. A third son of Sir Rowland de Boys, brother to Orlando and Oliver, brings news of Duke Frederick: he had set off with a military force against Duke Senior, but on the edge of the forest had met a hermit who converted him to a life of religious meditation; he has resigned his crown to Duke Senior, and restored the lands of the other exiles. They prepare for music and dancing, but Jaques will not stay: he is anxious to visit Duke Frederick, and to add to his store of experience by talking to him. Rosalind speaks an epilogue, in which she asks for the audience's approval of the play.

NOTES AND GLOSSARY:

compact is urged: agreement is clearly stated

desperate: dangerous

another flood . . . couples . . . ark: a reference to the biblical story of Noah's flood (Genesis 6.9–8.17). God destroyed the world by a flood, but saved Noah and his family. Noah built an ark (large covered floating vessel) into which he took his family. He also saved the world's fauna by taking into the ark every kind of living creature – seven of every clean creature, and two of every unclean creature (Genesis 7.2-3)

measure: stately dance

undone three tailors: ruined them (by not paying their bills)

copulatives: couples

marriage binds and blood breaks: a couple are bound by marriage-vows, but sexual desire (*blood*) may cause the breaking of these vows

how was that ta'en up?: how was that quarrel made up? Among gentlemen, a serious quarrel should result in a duel; Touchstone's account of his quarrel 'on the seventh cause' is a satire on courtiers who are afraid to fight and yet wish to save face

fool's bolt: there was a proverb, 'A fool's bolt is soon shot'. Touchstone is also punning on *quarrel*, which was the name for a cross-bow bolt

Countercheck: rebuke in reply to one received

in print: in a precise way, in exact order

Hymen: in classical mythology, the god of marriage, represented as a young man carrying a torch and veil

sure together: married

Juno's crown: Juno, the principal Roman goddess, was patroness of marriage and childbirth

In his own conduct: under his personal command

offerest fairly: bring a good gift

shrewd: irksome, harsh, ill-fortuned

With measure . . . measures fall: with your cup of joy filled to overflowing, begin dancing

have . . . cave: an exact rhyme: see note on *have . . . slave* (III.2.149–50) above

good wine . . . bush: sellers of wine hung green branches outside their shops

If I were a woman: the part of Rosalind would be played by a boy: see p. 18 in Part 1 above

bid me farewell: by applauding the play

Part 3

Commentary

Date

As You Like It was probably written in 1599. The first recorded reference to it occurs in August 1600, in the records of the Stationers' Company (the organisation of the London printers and booksellers). On the other hand, it is not mentioned in a list of Shakespeare's plays given by Francis Meres in his *Palladis Tamia*, published in 1598 (though admittedly Meres does not say that he is giving a complete list). In *As You Like It* (III.5.82) Shakespeare quotes a line from Christopher Marlowe's poem *Hero and Leander*, which was not published until 1598; on the other hand, there is evidence that the poem was circulating in manuscript before that date, and that Shakespeare knew it; and some scholars argue that Shakespeare would be more likely to refer to Marlowe as 'Dead Shepherd' (III.5.81) in 1593, immediately after his death, than in 1599. On general grounds of style and artistic maturity, however, 1599 seems a much more probable date than 1593, though some have argued that the play was written in 1593 and revised later.

Sources

The main source of the play is a prose romance by Thomas Lodge (c. 1558–1625) published in 1590, called *Rosalynde*. It was a popular work, being reprinted many times in the subsequent fifty years. From it, Shakespeare took the main incidents for *As You Like It*, but modified the material a good deal. For one thing, there was too much material for a play, and Shakespeare selected and compressed a great deal. In particular, he omitted many episodes of violence – brawls and battles. He also compressed the time-scale: for example, he makes the flight of Orlando and Adam to Arden take place at the same time as that of Celia and Rosalind, whereas in *Rosalynde* it takes place much later.

Shakespeare also rearranges the material. *Rosalynde* begins with Sir John of Bordeaux (the character corresponding to Sir Rowland de Boys). When he grows old, he tells his three sons what inheritance he is leaving to each, and lectures them on how they should behave after his death. He dies, and the eldest son then ill-treats the youngest, and ultimately deprives him of his inheritance. In *As You Like It*, all this is thrown into the past, and the action begins with the resulting quarrel between Orlando and Oliver.

There are also changes in the story. In *As You Like It*, Duke Frederick and Duke Senior are brothers, whereas the corresponding characters in *Rosalynde* are unrelated. By this change, Shakespeare introduces a parallel between the Oliver-Orlando story and the Frederick-Senior story. In both families there is cruel and unnatural behaviour between brothers; this suggests a general disorder in society, which is removed in the course of the play. The conversion of Duke Frederick at the end of the play is an invention of Shakespeare's: in Lodge, the corresponding character is killed in battle against his rival. This change again produces a symmetry in the play, since both wicked brothers (Oliver and Duke Frederick) undergo a sudden change of heart. Shakespeare emphasises this by making Oliver's change of heart much more sudden than Lodge does.

Above all, Shakespeare made changes in the characters. Lodge's Rosalynde is a conventional romance heroine, whereas Shakespeare's Rosalind is a character bursting with life. Shakespeare, moreover, invents many new characters, which have no counterparts in Lodge: these include William and Audrey, Jaques, and Touchstone. These characters give the play an entirely different thrust and direction from Lodge's romance. *Rosalynde* is a charming work, witty and elegant, but it is remote from real life, and wholly confined within the idealising conventions of Arcadian pastoral. *As You Like It*, on the other hand, uses the pastoral tradition, but is not confined within it.

The interacting traditions

Some of the changes made by Shakespeare to his source-material illustrate the interaction of the popular, learned, and courtly traditions. Lodge's romance is a sophisticated and courtly piece of writing. Nevertheless, the story of *Rosalynde*, with its series of dangerous adventures, its theme of constant love, its flight to the woods, and its changes of fortune, is very much the kind of romantic plot found in the popular dramatic tradition of the sixteenth century. In choosing this story, then, Shakespeare is following the popular tradition of comedy; but he transforms it under the influence of the courtly and academic traditions. These influences can be seen in the structure of the play: the old popular romantic comedies handled a series of episodes in straightforward chronological order, event after event; but, as we have seen, Shakespeare throws much of the story into the past, and in this is clearly influenced by classical theory and precedent. He also introduces pattern and structure into the play by means of parallel episodes and groups of characters, and in this he is almost certainly being influenced by the courtly prose-comedies of John Lyly (see p. 69) of the 1580s. As we have seen, Shakespeare introduces a parallelism between the

Orlando-Oliver plot and the Frederick-Senior plot, by making the two dukes into brothers, and by making both Oliver and Frederick undergo sudden conversions. The symmetrical grouping of characters is very clear in the case of the pairs of lovers: there are four pairs in the play, two of them courtly and two rustic, and they are contrasted in various ways; for example, the protracted wooing of Orlando and Rosalind contrasts amusingly with the lightning wooing of Oliver and Celia; and the simple-mindedness of Audrey is contrasted with the knowingness of Phebe.

The courtly and academic traditions also exercise a deep influence on the style of the play, both in its prose and in its verse. And the classical tradition lies behind one of the central concerns of the play, pastoralism: for the pastoral is a Greek and Latin literary mode. But what, in this context, do we mean by *pastoral*?

The pastoral tradition

Pastoral literature deals with the lives of shepherds. They are not real shepherds, however, but idealised figures living in a world of imagined innocence and simplicity: the pastoral world is Arcadian, a golden age remote from the troubles of real life. The shepherds are also poets, composing and singing their own songs: they sing love-songs to hard-hearted shepherdesses, they produce elegies for dead shepherds, they sing eulogies of great men, they have singing-competitions for prizes. The pastoral often has political, allegorical, or topical content below the surface, though it need not have. Pastoral, in fact, is very much country life as fondly imagined by the townsman, a projection of urban sophistication into an idealised rural setting, and the characters are courtiers or scholars dressed up in shepherds' clothes. There is no attempt to give a realistic depiction of rural life, an aim which is remote from the spirit of pastoral.

The pastoral tradition goes back to the *Idylls* of the Greek poet Theocritus (third century BC), whose pastoral poems were however still quite close to the realities of rural life in Sicily, where he was born. More influential on the European pastoral tradition were the *Eclogues* (pastoral poems) of the Latin poet Virgil (70–19 BC), which are remote from real country life, are set in an imaginary landscape, introduce supernatural characters, and evoke a Golden Age. They often have topical or allegorical significance – praising a patron, handling current political issues.

There was little pastoral during the Middle Ages, but with the rise of Renaissance humanism there came a revival of the tradition, and for several hundred years it was one of the most popular literary modes in Western Europe. In England, the revival of the pastoral began in the sixteenth century, and by Shakespeare's time there was a flood of pastoral writing. Besides eclogues in imitation of Virgil, such as Edmund Spenser's (?1552–99) *Shepherd's Calendar* (1579), there were pastoral dramas and long prose romances, both much influenced by continental models. The influence of Italian pastoral drama, containing mythological and allegorical elements, was transmitted to the English theatre by the comedies of Lyly, such as *Endymion* (1591). One of the influential prose romances, the *Diana* (1559) of Jorge de Montemayor (c. 1515–61), a Portuguese who wrote in Spanish, is perhaps referred to in *As You Like It* (IV.1.142); an English translation of *Diana* was published in 1598. One work much influenced by *Diana* was Sir Philip Sidney's (1554–86) *Arcadia*, part of which was published in 1590, but which had circulated in manuscript for some years before that date, and which was a powerful force in English literature. Lodge's *Rosalynde* is in the same tradition as the *Arcadia*: the long prose romance in which stories of chivalry are combined with pastoralism.

A critique of pastoralism?

Lodge's *Rosalynde* completely accepts the conventions of the pastoral, with all its unreality. In *As You Like It*, Shakespeare makes use of pastoral conventions, but the play is not confined within them, and indeed the play can be seen as a comment on the pastoral ideal.

Silvius and Phebe are conventional pastoral lovers of Renaissance literature – the pleading swain and hard-hearted shepherdess. Their language is that of courtly poetry (for example III.5.1–34). Phebe quotes a line from Marlowe (III.5.82), and when she falls in love with Ganymede she writes a conventional love-poem (IV.3.41–64). But Shakespeare introduces another country couple, William and Audrey, who have no counterparts in Lodge's romance. These are 'real' country characters. Audrey is an uneducated girl who does not know what *poetical* means (III.3.15), who is anxious to get married (V.3.3–5), and who abandons her rustic lover in favour of the courtly Touchstone (V.1.6–58). William is a country bumpkin, an almost speechless though good-humoured yokel. William and Audrey invariably talk in prose, whereas Silvius and Phebe always use verse. The presence of William and Audrey in the play is an implicit comment on the unnaturalness and conventionality of the pastoral lovers, Silvius and Phebe.

Between these two couples stand Rosalind and Orlando, and later Celia and Oliver. They are courtly, or at least gentle, characters who have escaped into the country, but they do not behave in the conventional pastoral way. Indeed, when Orlando does behave thus, by hanging love-poems on the trees (III.2.1–10), he is laughed at for his pains (III.2.92–153, 252–3, 344–9). Orlando and Rosalind provide a norm, a generous and human attitude to love which has neither the artificiality of pastoral nor the cynicism of Touchstone's marriage to Audrey. And the way in which Celia and Oliver fall in love and leap straight into one another's arms (V.2.1–40) is an amused comment on the long-drawn-out wooings of conventional pastoral.

Duke Senior, in his opening speech (II.1.1–17), praises life in the woods, contrasting it with 'painted pomp' and with the peril and the flattery of 'the envious court'; and Amiens chimes in with 'I would not change it' (II.1.18). But they do change it: at the end of the play, when their former rights are restored, the Duke and his followers (with the exception of Jaques) prepare with alacrity to return to their former life (V.4.148–95), and the Duke says that everyone who has 'endured shrewd days and nights' with him will share the benefit of his 'returned fortune' (V.4.170–1). There is thus an amusing contrast between the proclaimed joys of rural life, and the eagerness with which the exiles return to the court-life which they have so vilified. There is even a hint that the Duke and his followers perhaps indulge in fancy dress, putting on suitable clothes for their rustic parts. At their first appearance, they enter 'like foresters' (II.1.1 s.d.). This is unexceptionable, since men living in the forest must obviously wear appropriate clothing. But at the beginning of Act II Scene 7 they enter 'like outlaws'. There is at any rate a possibility that this indicates a change of clothes, that the exiles are playing games.

In justice to the Duke and his followers, however, it must be said that they acknowledge the hardships and discomforts of their life in the forest. The Duke refers to 'the penalty of Adam',

'the icy fang
And churlish chiding of the winter's wind.'
(II.1.6–7)

The advantage of forest-life over court-life is the absence of pomp and flattery, back-biting and hypocrisy. The winter wind, as one of the songs in the play says, is preferable to 'man's ingratitude' (II.7.177). But all the same they return to the court.

In pastoral, the writer (and the reader) are trying to have it both ways. They wish to enjoy the supposed simplicity, innocence, and freedom from anxiety of lower-class rural life, but simultaneously they wish to retain the advantages of being upper-class urban sophisticates with literary and artistic tastes. It has been suggested by C. L. Barber* that Touchstone makes fun of this contradiction at the heart of the pastoral convention in his apparently nonsensical speech telling Corin what he thinks of the life of a shepherd (III.2.13–20): he likes it because it is solitary, but dislikes it because it lacks company; he likes it because it is in the fields, but dislikes it because it is not in the court; and so on.

The overall effect of the play, however, is not to ridicule or satirise the

**Shakespeare's Festive Comedy*, Princeton University Press, 1959, p. 227.

pastoral convention: the pastoral passages have great charm, and the delights of country life are vividly evoked. Rather, the play sets the pastoral ideal in a wider context of attitudes, and gives a more inclusive view of human life; pastoralism is not destroyed, but we see it for what it is.

The Forest of Arden

The ideal world of pastoral owes something both to the classical idea of a Golden Age in the remote past, and to the Christian belief in the Garden of Eden (see p. 8 in Part 1 above). In the play, both ideas are linked with the Forest of Arden. In the very first mention of Arden, it is said that the Duke and his followers 'fleet the time carelessly as they did in the golden world' (I.1.111–12). In Duke Senior's first speech, he refers to 'the penalty of Adam' (II.1.5), reminding us of the Fall of Man and the Garden of Eden. From the start, therefore, Arden is associated with a primitive world of simplicity and innocence, in which man did not need to labour. There are also suggestions of timelessness about it, as when Orlando points out that there is 'no clock in the forest' (III.2.292–3), whereupon Rosalind gives a disquisition on the subjectivity of time (III.2.299–322).

Nominally, the Forest of Arden is in the Ardennes, a wooded mountain-range in north-eastern France, though the name also suggests the district of Arden in Warwickshire, near Shakespeare's home. Duke Senior and his followers live in the forest itself, apparently in caves (II.7.201), and hunt deer, while the shepherds live in the more open country on the edge of the forest, described by Rosalind as 'the skirts of the forest, like fringe upon a petticoat' (III.2.324–5). The landscape of Arden, however, is not that of any real place. There are elements which could be found in northern France or in England: the deer, the oak tree (II.1.31), the 'rank of osiers by the murmuring stream' (IV.3.80). But there are also olive-trees (IV.3.78) and even palm-trees (III.2.170–1); and the inhabitants of the forest include not only sheep and deer, but also a green-and-golden snake (IV.3.109) and a lioness (IV.3.115). Clearly the landscape belongs to the realm of fantasy.

But, even if Arden draws on visions of an ideal world, and resembles no known place, it is not merely an escape from real life. It is true that people flee to Arden from the cruelty of the world. The play opens outside Arden, in a world where cruelty, tyranny, and injustice reign, both at court and on the manor; and Arden provides a refuge from these evils. But it is not an easy refuge. It is not even easy to get there: Rosalind, Celia, and Touchstone, and then Orlando and Adam, and finally Oliver, all arrive in Arden in a state of physical exhaustion. And when people do get there, they are changed. The most striking examples of this are Oliver and Duke Frederick, who undergo religious conversions when they reach the forest. But more significant are the gradual changes that take place in people as a result of their experiences in Arden. For Arden is a place where people discover themselves, discover their own qualities and their own desires, often under stress; it is a place where, as Derek Traversi* has eloquently argued, basic human attitudes are put to the test, especially attitudes towards love and friendship.

Arden, then, is not a world of pastoral escapism, but a world of exploration and self-discovery; when the characters have achieved self-realisation there, they return to the outside world, which will be changed by their return.

Love

As is usual in Shakespeare's romantic comedies, love is one of the central themes of *As You Like It*. Various attitudes to love are contrasted. At one extreme is the conventional pastoral couple, Silvius and Phebe, with their highfalutin poetry, stock comparisons, and stereotyped attitudes. At the other extreme is the earthiness of Touchstone and Audrey: Audrey simply wants the status of a married woman (V.3.3–5), while for Touchstone marriage is no more than an outlet for sexual desire:

> 'As the ox hath his bow sir, the horse his curb, and the falcon her bells, so man hath his desires, and as pigeons bill, so wedlock would be nibbling.'
>
> (III.3.72–4)

The comparison with the ox, the horse, and the falcon, each with the mark of its servitude, suggests enslavement to sexuality at the simplest physical level.

Between these two couples stand Rosalind and Orlando, whose love is neither affected not lustful, but human and enriching, being based on a respect for the partner as a person. But we also see the education of Orlando as a lover. Rosalind's disguise causes the protractedness of their wooing; and Rosalind uses this wooing, not only to assure herself of the genuineness of Orlando's affection for her, but also to enlighten him about the true nature of love. At first, Orlando has many extravagant and conventional ideas about love: he runs through the forest hanging up love-poems (III.2.1–10), he thinks that love is eternal (IV.1.134), he believes that, if he is rejected, he will die (IV.1.84). Rosalind constantly undermines such extravagances and illusions with

***An Approach to Shakespeare: I. Henry VI to Twelfth Night*, 3rd ed., Hollis and Carter, London, 1968, p. 291.

her humour. When Orlando says that he will possess his love 'For ever and a day', she immediately ripostes with:

> 'Say "a day", without the "ever": no, no, Orlando, men are April when they woo, December when they wed: maids are May when they are maids, but the sky changes when they are wives.'
>
> (IV.1.135–8)

When he says that, if rejected, he will die, she replies by citing two famous lovers of antiquity (Troilus and Leander), and pointing out that, contrary to popular belief, they did not die of love; one was killed in battle, and the other was drowned. And she concludes, in a famous passage:

> 'But these are all lies: men have died from time to time, and worms have eaten them, but not for love.'
>
> (IV.1.96–8)

But this realistic attitude does not mean that Rosalind denies the power or the value of love. She herself is deeply in love with Orlando: her affection, she says, 'hath an unknown bottom, like the Bay of Portugal' (IV.1.192–3). But she wants love to be free from affectations and from illusions.

Rosalind's good-humoured attacks on the behaviour of lovers are not confined to Orlando. She ridicules the conventional appearance of a love-sick man (III.2.358–68), and is glad that Orlando is too sensible to conform. She describes the behaviour of a coquettish and capricious woman (III.2.391–9). She intervenes forcefully in the affair between Silvius and Phebe, rebuking Silvius for being a 'tame snake' (IV.3.71), and Phebe for her unkindness and lack of generosity (III.5.35–40). Indeed, this intervention proves effective, for it is Phebe's infatuation for 'Ganymede' that arouses her emotions and breaks down her self-centred coldness, so that her final ungrudging acceptance of Silvius (V.4.146–7) is by no means implausible.

Other themes

Various other themes are intertwined in the play. One of these is *friendship*. This is especially exemplified by Celia, who places her affection for Rosalind above her own political interests (I.3.75–80), promises to restore the dukedom to her after Frederick's death (I.2.16–20), and accompanies her to a dangerous exile when she is banished (I.3.92–136). Adam, similarly, is faithful to Orlando in adversity, and accompanies him into exile (II.3.1–76); but since the relationship between them is that of master and servant, this is perhaps an example of *faithfulness* rather than of friendship, although there is obviously great affection between the two men. Duke Senior's followers in Arden, similarly, place faithfulness to him above immediate advantage. In a world of tyranny and corruption, people of true integrity value personal bonds and traditional loyalties more highly than worldy gain, even though this may mean exile. In the end, the people who value love and friendship and loyalty return to the world outside Arden, and it is implied that the unnatural disorder seen earlier at court and on the gentleman's estate will now be overcome, and that the 'better world' which Le Beau had hoped for (I.2.273) will now be realised.

Another theme is the contrast between *Nature and Culture*. This appears right at the beginning of the play: one of Orlando's complaints against Oliver is that he has denied him a liberal education befitting a gentleman (I.1.4–14); but despite this lack of culture, Orlando's refined qualities shine through, and he is, as Oliver admits,

> 'gentle, never schooled, and yet learned, full of noble device, of all sorts enchantingly beloved.'
>
> (I.1.155–6)

What is suggested here is that heredity triumphs over environment: Orlando's gentle blood manifests itself in his qualities, despite his lack of education and the fact that he is made to keep company with menials (*hinds*, I.1.17). The theme of civilisation and nature is also seen in the contrast between the court and Arden; the civilisation of the court is corrupt, and has to be renewed by recourse to the world of nature.

The play also handles the contrast between *Nature and Fortune*. This was one of the commonplaces of the age, and it would be surprising if it were not mentioned in the play; but in fact it is discussed at some length in a debate between Rosalind and Celia (I.2.30–53). It is also exemplified in the characters who are carried downwards on Fortune's wheel (Duke Senior and his followers, Rosalind and Celia, Orlando) and then rely on the gifts of Nature (their inborn qualities) to survive 'the stubbornness of Fortune' (II.1.19).

Another theme is *Liberty and Licence*. When Rosalind and Celia flee to Arden, they go 'To liberty, and not to banishment' (I.3.136). But it is a strenuous liberty, one in which the characters achieve greater maturity. This liberty is contrasted with licence (the misuse of liberty), with which Duke Senior reproaches Jaques: the latter's invectives, the Duke says, are merely a disgorging on to the world of the evils which he has caught 'with licence of free foot' (II.7.68).

Finally, there is a *seasonal theme* in the play. Almost the first thing mentioned by Duke Senior is 'the seasons' difference' (II.1.6), and the main hardship in Arden is the winter wind (II.1.7, II.7.175), winter and rough weather (II.5.8). But one song in the play evokes springtime, the time of bird-song and love-making (V.3.15–32); this comes near the end of the play, whereas the evocation of winter occurs especially in Act II, so that there is a suggestion in the play of a transition from winter to spring – from the winter of hardship and tyranny to the spring of 'returned fortune' (V.4.171).

Songs and masque

Songs play a considerable part in *As You Like It*. There are five songs in the play, not counting a snatch sung by Touchstone (III.3.89–95). Five songs in a play is a large number by Shakespeare's standards: two of his plays contain six songs each, and one other play contains five, but the remainder contain fewer than five, and about half the plays contain no songs at all. On the functions of the songs, see the specimen essay in Part 4 below, pp. 81–3.

One of the songs forms part of a masque (a short formal and spectacular entertainment in which the spectators often played a part). In the masque in *As You Like It* (V.4.105–43), a person representing Hymen (god of marriage) enters with Celia and Rosalind, whose true identity is thus revealed, and pairs off the various lovers. The language of the masque is different from the surrounding dialogue, being rhymed and in short lines. This sets it apart as a solemn ritual, a moment of formal decision and commitment before the wedding festivities which are to follow. To a modern audience it seems strange and artificial, but the Elizabethans were accustomed to masques, and would have taken it in their stride as an appropriately ritualistic way of untying the knots of the play, pairing off the lovers, and preparing for the happy ending. The masque, moreover, by its very lack of realism, makes the surrounding play seem more real.

The characters

Once the action of the play moves to the Forest of Arden, there is very little plot. There are episodes and incidents, debates and jokes, atmosphere and song; but the main movement forward of the plot is halted until Oliver and Duke Frederick arrive in the forest. Because of this absence of plot, the play relies a good deal on characterisation. Nevertheless, it contains relatively little soliloquy. Characters seldom analyse themselves, or brood on their problems. There are no inner struggles, and the character-changes that take place in Oliver and in Duke Frederick are sudden ones, with no preceding inner struggle or self-doubt. Characters in the play reveal their nature, not by self-communing, but by interaction with other characters, in dialogue and action.

Rosalind

Rosalind is the central character of the play, and speaks more than a quarter of its words. Her attitude to love provides a yardstick by which we judge the other characters. Although she rejects the illusions of love, she accepts love, when it comes to her, with complete naturalness and spontaneity. Nor does she show any prudery or false bashfulness; when Celia asks her whether all of her melancholy is for her father, she replies:

'No, some of it is for my child's father.'

(I.3.11)

She means, plainly, the man she wishes to marry and have a child by; she is completely honest in recognising her desires.

Rosalind has enormous energy and ebullience. This is seen in her constant flow of talk: when she is in full spate, it is difficult for other characters to get a word in. When Celia brings the news that Orlando is in the forest (III.2.167–243), Rosalind interrupts so frequently that Celia can hardly tell her story, and has to protest to get a hearing ('Give me audience', 'Cry holla to thy tongue', 'I would sing my song without a burden'). At the least provocation, Rosalind will launch into a witty disquisition – on Time (III.2.294–322), on the conventional marks of a lover (III.2.358–68), on the affectations of men who travel abroad (IV.1.29–36), and so on. Her humour is infectious and seemingly without end, and she mocks and teases Orlando continually, often with little throw-away lines which deflate his solemnity, such as 'Fridays and Saturdays and all' (IV.1.105–6) and 'Ay, and twenty such' (IV.1.108). She also turns her wit on any other character available – Le Beau (I.2.88–133), Touchstone (III.2.111–16), Jaques (IV.1.1–26), Silvius (IV.3.20–75). Her wit is, however, good-natured, and never malicious. It is true that she is very sharp with Phebe, but this is because she sees a moral weakness in her that calls for correction.

It is especially after the flight to Arden that Rosalind's exuberant humour flowers. At court, she has bouts of wit with Celia (I.2.23–54, I.3.1–35), but is more subdued than she becomes later. At her first appearance, she is melancholy, and Celia is trying to cheer her up (I.2.1–13); and at her next appearance she is silent, and has to be urged to talk by Celia (I.3.1–6). The second of these occurrences is clearly due to her sudden love for Orlando, but the first is because of her father's banishment and the difficulty of her position at court. She accepts this position without affectation, and there is a complete lack of constraint in her relationship with Celia. When Duke Frederick accuses her of being a traitor, she defends herself with dignity, self-control, and patent sincerity (I.3.39–63). When the sentence of banishment is passed, she is, not surprisingly, depressed; and once again it falls to Celia to comfort her. But from the moment that she thinks of the idea of disguising herself as a man, her spirits rise, and thereafter she is full of vitality and humour.

It is in Arden that Rosalind displays her practical ability, her efficiency as an organiser. It is she who has the idea of buying the sheepcote (II.4.88–90). When Orlando appears in Arden, she takes the initiative and accosts him (III.2.287–91), and by the end of the scene has thought of the mock-wooing game, which ensures that she will have frequent contact with him. She intervenes vigorously in the Silvius-Phebe wooing (III.5.35–63), and plays a controlling role in the resulting complications. Above all, she organises the final compact between the lovers (V.2.104–18, V.4.5–25), and the masque of Hymen which unravels all the knots (V.4.105–43).

At court, however, it is Celia who takes the initiative: she suggests their joint flight (I.3.94–103), proposes the Forest of Arden as their goal (I.3.105), and answers the doubting Rosalind's objections with the suggestion that they shall disguise themselves 'in poor and mean attire' (I.3.109). It is then that Rosalind has her idea of dressing up as a man (I.3.112–20), and her imagination is fired. She at once perks up, and enters into the scheme with enthusiasm; and indeed it is she that makes the final suggestion that they should take Touchstone with them.

Rosalind's disguise is of central importance in the play. It makes possible the protracted wooing with Orlando, which would offer little dramatic interest if it were conducted straight. The wooing offers many opportunities for humour, especially through dramatic irony. This is the effect achieved when the audience has knowledge which is hidden from some of the characters on the stage, so that utterances can have meanings of which those characters are unaware. Orlando does not know that Ganymede, whom he is wooing under the name of Rosalind, really is Rosalind, and this produces dramatic irony, as when Rosalind assures him: 'By my life, she will do as I do' (IV.1.147). Similar effects are achieved in the relationship between Rosalind and Phebe, as when Rosalind promises to marry her if she remains willing (V.4.11); the audience knows that Phebe has walked into a trap. Moreover, disguise has a liberating effect on Rosalind, since it permits her to say things which a woman would not normally say; she becomes much more free-spoken in her humour, for example in her satirical remarks about women, as Celia complains (IV.1.186–9). Indeed, this freedom no doubt explains the enthusiasm and delight with which Rosalind embarks on her masculine role.

Orlando

Orlando is very young: he is twice called 'boy' (I.1.49, 161); Rosalind remarks on his lack of beard (III.2.362); before the wrestling, Celia says that he is too young (I.2.143), and the Duke wishes to dissuade him from the contest because of his youth (I.2.148–50). His revolt against Oliver can be seen as the result of his first coming to manhood, and his realisation of his position. When the princesses approach him before the wrestling, he speaks feelingly of his situation, as one without friends and without a place in the world (I.2.171–80); Rosalind's reply suggests that this has struck a sympathetic chord with her, she too being one with no place in the world. After the wrestling, when the princesses speak to him again, Orlando is tongue-tied, partly because Rosalind has swept him off his feet, partly because he lacks practice in the arts of courtly conversation with ladies. Even when Rosalind returns and gives him another chance to speak to her, he is silent, and recognises that it is because passion hangs weights upon his tongue (I.2.246). Subsequently, it is Rosalind's disguise that enables him to express his affection for her, since he believes that he is speaking to a stranger.

In fighting Charles, Orlando shows his physical strength and courage. In confronting Oliver and demanding his rights, he has already shown his moral courage. These qualities appear in his later actions – the comforting of Adam (II.6.4–17), his attempt to obtain food for Adam by force (II.7.88–100), his rescue of Oliver from the lioness (IV.3.99–133). In this last incident, Orlando hesitates: twice he turns away, intending to leave his brother to his fate, but it is 'nature, stronger than his just occasion' that finally prompts him to risk his life for his enemy (IV.3.130). In making this crucial moral choice, Orlando is guided by nature: that is, by his innate gentility, the generous qualities he has inherited, and by the natural ties of kinship.

Despite his lack of formal education, Orlando knows how a lover is expected to behave: he hangs mediocre love-poems on the trees, and talks of the eternity of his love, and of dying if he is rejected. He agrees to Rosalind's mock-wooing because he wants an opportunity to 'be talking of her' (IV.1.82), but in the end he finds this unsatisfying, for he 'can live no longer by thinking' (V.2.48); and this confession prompts Rosalind to unfold to him her proposal to produce his love to him by means of magic arts (V.2.49–65).

Celia

Celia is affectionate and unmercenary, placing her love for Rosalind above worldly advantage. She is competent and practical: she takes the initiative in planning the flight to Arden, she persuades Touchstone to accompany them, and she thinks of crucial things like taking their money and jewels and evading pursuit (I.3.130–5). She is less ebullient than Rosalind, quieter and more detached, but she is quite capable of teasing her, as when she holds back the identity of the person who has hung up the love-poems in the forest (III.2.173–205). She is also witty, and holds her own against Rosalind in their repartee. In her own quiet and amused way, she can also undermine Rosalind, as when she playfully suggests that Orlando is not in love (III.4.19–41), and laughs at his brave verses, brave words, and brave oaths, adding that 'all's brave that youth mounts and folly guides' (III.4.36–41); or, when Rosalind goes to sigh in the shade until Orlando comes, replies laconically 'And I'll sleep' (IV.1.203). Here she is doing for Rosalind what Rosalind does for others: preventing her from going to absurd extremes by making satirical comment. It is Celia's very demureness and rationality which make so amusing her sudden passion for Oliver, which is made even more amusing by Rosalind's characteristically florid account (V.2.28–39). In the source-material, Celia has a strong motive for loving Oliver, since he rescues her from outlaws; Shakespeare instead gives us the instantaneous love and the whirlwind wooing, obtaining maximum contrast with the Orlando-Rosalind affair.

Jaques

Jaques takes no part in the action of the play: he is an outsider, a commentator. This does not mean, however, that his comments on people and events are necessarily Shakespeare's own. Jaques is addicted to two things which were fashionable around 1600: satire and melancholy. Melancholy was believed to be caused by a lack of balance in the 'humours' in the body, and was a common pose around the turn of the century. Jaques is proud of his melancholy, which he claims is a unique variety, 'a melancholy of mine own, compounded of many simples' (IV.1.15–16); he obviously enjoys it. One of the sources of his melancholy is the contemplation of his travels: he has sought after experience, and it has made him sad (IV.1.17–23). Rosalind laughs at him for this: she says that he has sold his lands in order to see other men's, and so has 'rich eyes and poor hands' (IV.1.19–26).

Jaques's satire is linked to his melancholy, for it arises from his low opinion of human beings. He is a cynic, always assuming the lowest motives in people, and seeing only what is absurd in them. His famous 'Seven Ages of Man' (II.7.140–67) is witty, but it is a caricature, seeing only what is ridiculous. As has often been pointed out, its superficiality is immediately shown up by the entry of Orlando carrying Adam: in Jaques's account of life, there is no place for the self-effacing loyalty, affection, and courage shown by these two. The Duke attacks Jaques's satirical habits, and suggests that they are merely an expression of his earlier licentious life (II.7.65–9). In reply, Jaques does not answer this charge: his defence is that he does not attack individuals; his satire is general, and if an individual takes offence he is really accusing himself

(II.7.70–87). Amiens says that Jaques's satire pierces the body of 'country, city, court', and that he also attacks their own life in Arden, where they are usurpers and tyrants (II.1.58–63). In fact we hear very little from Jaques either on country life or on the life of the exiles in Arden. He does indeed parody Amiens's song 'Under the greenwood tree', suggesting that men are asses and fools to leave their wealth and ease in favour of life in the forest (II.5.47–54). But the other satirical shafts that we hear from him concern the hard-heartedness and self-interest of 'fat and greasy citizens' (II.1.55–7); the extravagant and indecorous clothes of the wives of rich citizens (II.7.74–8); the extravagant clothes of some men of humble rank (II.7.79–82); the folly of being in love (III.2.246–86); and what he calls *compliment* (II.5.22–7) – ceremony, the giving of thanks, polite phrases – which is characteristic of the court rather than of the country. The function of Jaques in the play, therefore, is not just to parody pastoralism, or to laugh at the exiles in Arden. His presence does however bring a caustic and critical voice into the play, inviting the audience to question people and events, not to accept anything too easily.

Jaques is, however, rather self-satisfied about his critical role. He is convinced that he knows better than anybody else, and he wishes to 'Cleanse the foul body of th'infected world' (II.7.60). But he never shows any signs of *self*-criticism. In this he differs from Orlando, who, when invited to join in invective against the world, replies:

> 'I will chide no breather in the world but myself, against whom I know most faults.'
>
> (III.2.272–3)

In fact in Jaques's attacks on the world there is something self-regarding and self-indulgent.

Nevertheless, Jaques is a sympathetic character. He is lively, and often genuinely witty. Moreover, his interest in 'experience' is not a pose, but is real. Despite his assumed melancholy, he is for ever interested in people and events, and has a great appetite for life. This is seen in his obvious delight at meeting Touchstone in the forest, an encounter which produces in him a great outburst of mirth (II.7.12–43); and the same delight is seen again later, when he introduces Touchstone to the Duke, and is clearly taken up with Touchstone's qualities, and is not at all thinking about himself (V.4.35–104). He eavesdrops on Touchstone and Audrey out of insatiable curiosity; but he intervenes in their proposed marriage, not to moralise, but to give them good and sensible advice (III.3.71–85). At the end of the play, typically, he refuses to return to the proffered good fortune at court, and instead goes off to talk to the converted Duke Frederick, to add to his stock of experience (V.4.177–82).

Touchstone

Touchstone is also a commentator, but very different from Jaques: the one is a melancholy, blasé man of the world, the other a professional jester. Touchstone's name indicates his function: he tests the value or genuineness of things, and so shows up folly and insincerity and affectation. There is some doubt whether Touchstone is his real name, or is simply a pseudonym which he assumes in Arden: in the First Folio text he is most often called 'Clown', but the stage-direction at the beginning of Act II Scene 4 reads 'Enter Rosaline for Ganymede, Celia for Aliena, and Clown *alias* Touchstone'.

Many streams contribute to the Clown of Shakespearean comedy, including the parasite or buffoon of classical drama, the Vice of medieval drama (who was a comic character), and the Lord of Misrule in English folk-festivals, especially those of Christmas. Above all, however, the stage-clown reflects the professional Court Fool. The Court Fool was a servant at court or in a great household who was kept for the entertainment of the lord. He was a privileged person, and could speak truths and make criticisms that nobody else would dare to mention. There were two different types of Fool, the 'natural' and the 'artificial'; the former was a genuine imbecile, kept in the household as a butt and laughing-stock; the latter was a professional jester masquerading as an imbecile. In either case the Fool would wear the standard uniform – a long gown made of 'motley', a woollen cloth of mixed colours.

Some critics have said that Touchstone is presented inconsistently, sometimes being an idiot and sometimes a shrewd jester; it has even been suggested that he changes from one to the other on reaching Arden. In fact there is no real inconsistency. Nothing is proved by the fact that Touchstone is referred to as 'dull' (I.2.52), 'natural' (I.2.51), 'clownish' (I.3.128), and 'roynish' (II.2.8): part of the technique of the professional jester was to use the pretence of imbecility as a mask for his satirical sallies. Indeed, Duke Senior comments on this technique in Touchstone:

> 'He uses his folly like a stalking-horse, and under the presentation of that he shoots his wit.'
>
> (V.4.103–4)

Nor is there any real change when Touchstone moves to Arden: at court, at his first appearance in the play, it is already clear that he is not an idiot, and that he has a satirical wit, as in his account of the knight who swore by his honour that the pancakes were good (I.2.61–76). It is simply that, when he gets to Arden, there are more targets for ridicule.

One of Touchstone's favourite methods of ridicule is parody, and he constantly parodies the behaviour and attitudes of other people. The behaviour of lovers is parodied in his account of his wooing of Jane Smile (II.4.42–51). He improvises a parody of Orlando's love-verses (III.2.97–108). In his debate with Corin on court-life and country-life, he parodies the methods of academic disputation (III.2.38–42). In his putting-down of William, he parodies the techniques of rhetoric (V.1.39–56). He ridicules the code of honour and the rules for quarrelling, in his account of the degrees of the lie (V.4.66–100). He satirises courtiers, presenting evidence that he himself has been one:

> 'I have trod a measure, I have flattered a lady, I have been politic with my friend, smooth with mine enemy, I have undone three tailors, I have had four quarrels, and like to have fought one'.
>
> (V.4.43–46)

He is indeed a very learned Fool. He is particularly well-versed in logic, which he delights in perverting for his own ends, as when he proves that Corin is damned (III.2.30–42), or that Audrey ought not to be chaste (III.3.22–33), or that the knight was not forsworn (I.2.61–76).

Touchstone's habit of parody shades off into play-acting. In Arden, he puts on the airs of a great courtier, and is addressed by Corin as '*Master* Touchstone' (III.2.11–12), a title reserved for the gentry. The playing of a part is especially obvious when Jaques comes forward and offers to help in the marriage ceremony with Audrey, whereupon Touchstone in reply adopts the behaviour of a great man (III.3.67–70).

Touchstone ridicules the pastoral ideal and the glorification of country life. One of his first comments on arriving in Arden is:

> 'Ay, now am I in Arden, the more fool I, when I was at home I was in a better place.'
>
> (II.4.13–14)

This is an apt counterbalance to Amiens's sentiment, 'I would not change it' (II.1.18). Touchstone's longest piece on the subject is his discussion with Corin on the relative merits of court life and country life, in which his nimble wit makes circles round the shepherd (III.2.11–81).

Although Touchstone is primarily a commentator, he also plays some part in the action. He and Audrey form one of the contrasted sets of couples in the play. For Touchstone, marriage is captivity, entered into only under the pressure of sexual desire. The point about captivity emerges in his reference to the ox's bow (yoke), the horse's curb, and the falcon's bells (III.3.72–4): these are all marks of these creatures' servitude to man. Touchstone enters the servitude of marriage with some reluctance, and has an eye on a later possible escape from it (III.3.81–4). It will be observed, however, that even Touchstone's participation in the action of the play constitutes some kind of comment on the behaviour of other characters.

Other characters

Phebe and Silvius are conventional lovers of Renaissance literature: the cold woman and the faithful complaining man. Phebe is unscrupulous and deceitful: she makes use of Silvius to carry her letter to Ganymede, and lies to him about its contents. Rosalind says that she is not even beautiful (though this may be part of her therapy).

Phebe writes poetry, but Audrey, the real country girl, does not know the meaning of the word 'poetical' (III.3.15). Like Phebe, she spurns her local lover in favour of an attractive outsider. She is, however 'honest' (III.3.22–35), which is why Touchstone has to marry her. William, who appears in only one scene (V.1), is good-natured but stupid. He has few words, but is polite and good-tempered.

Corin is a rural character who is neither a pastoral stereotype nor a yokel. He is simple, dignified, and sensible. He is unambitious and is satisfied with his way of life, but he indulges in no extravagant praise of rural bliss, and deplores the churlish disposition of his master, who is inhospitable (II.4.77–9): even in Arden, we learn, there are bad masters. Corin has much in common with Adam, who possesses old-fashioned virtues – thrift, honesty, loyalty. Orlando remarks that Adam's virtues belong to a previous age, 'When service sweat for duty, not for meed' (II.3.58); and part of Adam's function is to show up the degeneracy of the age by suggesting what it had been like earlier, when Orlando's father was alive (I.1.77–9). Once they arrive in Arden, Adam disappears from the action.

Oliver and Duke Frederick are both straightforward portraits of unscrupulous and suspicious tyrants. They both behave unnaturally towards a brother, and have no objects except wealth and power. The self-destructive nature of such qualities is nicely shown when Duke Frederick seizes Oliver's possessions and sends him off to find Orlando: the larger pike swallows the smaller. There follows an exquisite touch: Oliver protests that he had never loved his brother in his life, to which Duke Frederick makes the hypocritical but unanswerable reply 'More villain thou' (III.1.14–15).

Amiens and the other followers of Duke Senior have rejected the tyranny of Frederick, preferring exile in the woods with the legitimate duke. Duke Senior himself does not give an unqualified praise of their rural life: he knows that it is 'adversity' (II.1.12), but he contrasts it with the evils of court life. His attitude is one of dignified and philosophical acceptance of misfortune, as Amiens suggests:

> 'happy is your Grace,
> That can translate the stubbornness of fortune
> Into so quiet and so sweet a style.'
>
> (II.1.18–20)

His manner contrasts sharply with Frederick's: the latter blusters and hectors, but Duke Senior always speaks graciously and with self-control; this is even seen when he rebukes Orlando for bursting in violently on them (II.7.92–4). He is a shrewd judge of people, penetrating to the motives of Jaques's satire (II.7.64–9) and showing an immediate appreciation of the qualities of Touchstone (V.4.61, 103–4). His fortitude, self control, and magnanimity are such that the audience is confident at the end of the play that his return to the court will transform it.

Prose and verse

The play is partly in prose, and partly in verse. Prose predominates: there are over 12,000 words of prose to about 9,000 words of verse. This is a high proportion of prose for a Shakespeare play: in only three other plays is there more prose than verse, and in most of the plays there is considerably more verse than prose. On the other hand, *As You Like It* is not the most extreme case: in *The Merry Wives of Windsor* there is seven times as much prose as verse.

In *As You Like It*, prose tends to be used for scenes of low emotional tension, and for the speech of characters of low social status. Verse is used by high-ranking characters, especially when speaking formally, and for situations of high emotion or of great moment. Duke Frederick and Duke Senior almost invariably speak verse, and when they do so the characters around them follow suit. By contrast, Touchstone invariably speaks prose, even when the characters around him speak verse, and in Act II Scene 4 the writing fluctuates between verse and prose, according to whether Touchstone is involved or not. There are other characters who invariably speak prose: Charles the wrestler, William, Audrey; this is clearly because of their low social status. Silvius and Phebe, on the other hand, invariably speak in verse, because, although nominally they are of low social status, in fact they are conventional pastoral figures, and their more literary language clearly distinguishes them from William and Audrey. Corin, too, usually speaks in verse, and so is marked as a 'pastoral' character; the only exception is his discussion with Touchstone (III.2.11–83), which is in prose. This exception is not surprising: the influence of Touchstone is so powerful that anybody talking to him speaks prose; even Duke Senior slips into prose for three short speeches when Touchstone is holding the centre of the stage (V.4.52, 61, 103–4).

Some characters, then, are normally verse-speakers, and others prose-speakers. The remaining characters fluctuate between verse and prose. To some extent, their choice is influenced by other speakers. Jaques often speaks prose, but in Act II Scene 7, where Duke Senior holds court, he uses verse, like the rest of the characters. Rosalind and Celia most often speak prose, but switch to verse when they talk with Corin (III.4.42–54), or Silvius (IV.3.7–40), or Phebe (V.2.72–100). But the choice of prose or verse is also influenced by the emotional pitch of the scene. Low-keyed scenes, like Act II Scene 5 and Act IV Scene 2, are in prose. Orlando speaks verse when he runs through the wood in a love-frenzy hanging up his poems (III.2.1–10), but later in the scene converses with Jaques and with Rosalind in prose. In the first scene of the play, Oliver speaks prose, but when he arrives in Arden he uses verse to tell Celia and Rosalind the solemn news of his conversion and of the battle with the lioness (IV.3.76–157). Verse is used, similarly, for the conversation between Celia and Rosalind after the pronouncement of banishment (I.3.88–136).

The prose

One thing which the academic and courtly traditions brought into the public theatre was style. The writing in the old popular tradition was somewhat artless; the more learned writers brought self-conscious art. Shakespeare's prose was influenced by Latin writers, such as Cicero, but also by an English stylist John Lyly (*c.* 1554–1606), who wrote a prose romance called *Euphues* (1579), and then, in the 1580s, a series of elegant prose comedies for courtly audiences. For a time, Lyly's elaborate and artificial prose style made his works the rage in literary circles. He used symmetrical sentences with balanced structures – clause balanced against clause, phrase against phrase, word against word – the balance often being reinforced by strong alliteration. He used numerous illustrative comparisons, which produced elegant images, but which tended to be decorative rather than illuminating, introduced for their own sake. Shakespeare's prose is less mannered, and the antitheses and symmetries in it are less obvious and predictable. The following is a piece of serious prose from *As You Like It:*

> 'I beseech you, punish me not with your hard thoughts, wherein I confess me much guilty to deny so fair and excellent ladies anything. But let your fair eyes and gentle wishes go with me to my trial; wherein if I be foiled, there is but one shamed that was never gracious: if killed, but one dead that is willing to be so: I shall do my friends no wrong, for I have none to lament me: the world no injury, for in it I have nothing: only in the world I fill up a place, which may be better supplied, when I have made it empty.'
>
> (I.2.171–80)

There we see balanced phrases – *fair eyes* answered by *gentle wishes.* Whole clauses are symmetrically deployed: (a) *if I be foiled . . . one shamed . . . never gracious*, (b) *if killed . . . one dead . . . willing to be so*; the two *if*–clauses, clearly, have parallel structures. A similar symmetry is seen in (a) *my friends no wrong, for I have none to lament me*, (b) *the world no injury, for in it I have nothing*. The symmetry, however, never becomes mechanical: for example, *willing to be so* provides a satisfying counterpart to *never gracious*, but could not have been predicted from it, and has a different grammatical structure. Alliteration occurs, but it is not obvious, as it often is in Lyly, and moreover it seems natural and functional: *no . . . none . . . no . . . nothing* (the alliteration reinforcing the negatives which are central to what Orlando is saying). Nor are there any of the decorative comparisons so common in Lyly's prose. The effect of the syntactic patterning in Orlando's speech is to make it lucid and easy to follow, but also to make it sound considered and beautifully poised.

Often, the prose of the play is much more conversational, as in the following exchange between Rosalind and Orlando:

> *Ros.* Nay, you might keep that check for it, till you met your wife's wit going to your neighbour's bed.
> *Orl.* And what wit could wit have to excuse that?
> *Ros.* Marry, to say she came to seek you there: you will never take her without her answer, unless you take her without her tongue: O, that woman that cannot make her fault her husband's occasion, let her never nurse her child herself, for she will breed it like a fool.
> *Orl.* For these two hours, Rosalind, I will leave thee.
> *Ros.* Alas, dear love, I cannot lack thee two hours.
> *Orl.* I must attend the Duke at dinner, by two o'clock I will be with thee again.
> *Ros.* Ay, go your ways, go your ways: I knew what you would prove, my friends told me as much, and I thought no less: that flattering tongue of yours won me: 'tis but one cast away, and so, come death: two o'clock is your hour?
> *Orl.* Ay, sweet Rosalind.
>
> (IV.1.156–73)

There, Shakespeare gives the illusion of real informal speech by inserting the exclamations, utterance-initiators, terms of address, and petty oaths found in conversation: *Nay, Marry, O, Rosalind, Alas, dear love, Ay.* He uses forms typical of the spoken language (*'tis* for *it is*) and colloquial expressions *(go your ways)*. He keeps the sentence-structure simple: there are only three subordinate clauses in the passage, and most of its sentences are either minor ones (not having a subject and predicate) or are simple ones (having a main clause but no subordinate clauses). The simple sentences may be strung together without any conjunction, as in Orlando's third speech. On the other hand, the prose lacks the repetitions, changes of construction, and incoherences of real informal speech; for a reproduction of such features on the stage would make the dialogue slow, confusing, monotonous, and boring. Shakespeare gives the illusion of informal speech, but gives the sentences enough structure and pattern for them to be clear and interesting to the listener.

The verse

If we leave aside the songs and the masque of Hymen (which is set apart by a metre of its own), the verse of the play is blank verse, that is, unrhymed iambic pentameter. An English iambic pentameter has the following basic pattern:

U / U / U / U / U /
But fare / thee well, / thou art / a gal- / lant youth

(I.2.217)

The line consists of five metrical units (called *feet*) each consisting of an unstressed syllable followed by a stressed one. On this basic pattern the poet makes variations, and may depart quite a long way from it. Two common variations are the inversion of a foot, and the use of a foot consisting of two unstressed syllables. Both are seen in this line:

/ U U / U / U U U /
Which of / the two / was daught- / -er of / the Duke

(I.2.258)

There the first foot is inverted, and the fourth foot consists of two unstressed syllables. In his later plays, Shakespeare often uses very free rhythms in his blank verse, but in *As You Like It* the variations are never so great as to obscure the underlying pattern, though they are sufficient to give considerable rhythmic variety to the verse.

Occasionally, rhyme is used. Particularly common is the use of a rhymed couplet at the end of a scene, giving a sense of finality. Sometimes, a rhymed couplet occurs elsewhere, as when Phebe says:

'Dead Shepherd, now I find thy saw of might,
"Who ever loved, that loved not at first sight?".'

(III.5.81–2)

Here the rhyme gives a neat, pointed quality, suitable for a 'saw'. In Orlando's exalted speech at the beginning of Act III Scene 2, a more complicated rhyme-pattern is used.

Rhetoric

Writers in Shakespeare's time were much influenced by the theories of classical rhetoric. Handbooks of rhetoric dealt with numerous topics – the finding of material, its arrangement, style, memorisation of a speech, delivery, gesture. In literature, it is in matters of style that rhetorical influence is most obvious; and especially popular with late sixteenth-century writers were the figures of speech. Figures were defined as departures from normal usage for artistic effect, and covered an enormous range of different things, from the smallest stylistic detail (such as the use of a non-normal variant of a single word) to the mode within which a passage, or even a whole work, operated (such as imprecation). There are two main types of figure, Tropes and Schemes. In tropes there is some kind of substitution or transfer of meaning; words are used in a meaning which is not their usual one, the basic type being metaphor; they include irony and allegory. Schemes are figures in which there is no such substitution or transfer of meaning. In Grammatical Schemes the normal linguistic rules are broken (for instance, by non-normal word-order, or by breaking off a sentence and leaving it unfinished). In Rhetorical Schemes there is no such breaking of the rules of grammar or syntax; they cover many different things, including verbal patterns (obtained by repetition) and elaborate set-pieces (for instance, descriptions of people or places).

Late sixteenth-century poets loved the figures, and so did their readers. Handbooks were written defining and illustrating them, and the number of different figures described could run to a hundred and fifty or more. In the 1580s and 1590s, poets made lavish use of figures of all kinds, but they were especially fond of Rhetorical Schemes, and in particular the ones which consisted of verbal patterns. Shakespeare is no exception, and in his earliest works he makes great use of figures, often very elaborate ones. By the time he wrote *As You Like It* he had moved away from the more obvious figures found in his earliest works, and favoured subtler and less obtrusive ones, but he could still use Rhetorical Schemes of repetition, as in the following lines spoken by Orlando:

> 'If ever you have looked on better days:
> If ever been where bells have knolled to church:
> If ever sat at any good man's feast:
> If ever from your eyelids wiped a tear,
> And known what 'tis to pity . . .'

(II.7.114–18)

Here the pattern consists in starting a series of lines with the same two words, and its effect is to make Orlando's request into a solemn adjuration. The Duke continues the pattern by repeating Orlando's phrases in his reply (II.7.121–7), and this suggests the harmony and sympathy now established between the two speakers. The formal patterns of the whole passage evoke a sense or order and ritual, reinforcing what is said about the civilised life, and contrasting strongly with what precedes (Orlando bursting in violently, sword drawn, on what he believes is a band of brigands).

Figures are used as much in the prose of the play as in the verse, and a different figure of repetition is seen in the following lines of Rosalind's:

> 'For your brother and my sister no sooner met, but they looked: no sooner looked, but they loved: no sooner loved, but they sighed: no sooner sighed, but they asked one another the reason: no sooner knew the reason, but they sought the remedy: and in these degrees, they have made a pair of stairs to marriage, which they will climb incontinent, or else be incontinent before marriage.'
>
> (V.2.31–8)

The main figure here is the one called *gradatio*, which is a pattern of the type A-B/B-C/C-D/D-E, etc. (*met . . . looked/looked . . . loved/loved . . . sighed/sighed . . . reason . . .*). The figure is here used for humorous effect, to describe the rapid and seemingly inevitable sequence of events in the wooing of Celia and Oliver. There are several other figures in the passage, including alliteration, and the giving of a sequence of events dependent on one another, and the pun on *incontinent*. There is also a concealed pun in *stairs*, for the literal meaning of Latin *gradatio* is 'series of steps, staircase': Rosalind deliberately chooses the rhetorical figure which will represent the series of steps which Celia and Oliver have taken.

We have seen that Touchstone is a master of logic, and he is also a master of rhetoric, which he often uses for parodistic purposes. The following is an example from his scene with William:

> 'Therefore you clown abandon (which is in the vulgar "leave") the society (which in the boorish is "company") of this female (which in the common is "woman"): which together, is "abandon the society of this female", or clown thou perishest: or to thy better understanding, diest; or (to wit) I kill thee, make thee away, translate thy life into death, thy liberty into bondage.'
>
> (V.1.46–52)

Here Touchstone uses the figure *Synonymia*; for the benefit of the ignorant William, he translates his fine words (*abandon, society, female*) into everyday equivalents, and then gives a series of synonyms for *perish* (as though he was proposing to kill William six times over). The aim is to dumbfound the unfortunate William, but at the same time Touchstone is making fun of people who use pompous language.

The examples of figures so far given have been fairly obvious large-scale ones, but the play is full of less obtrusive ones: every witty reply, every joke, every pun, every piece of chop-logic, every self-correction in phraseology, every balanced sentence, contains a figure of some kind, and often several. Nevertheless, the more obvious large-scale figures do play a prominent part in the play. It contains many set-pieces, some of which constitute figures themselves, and all of which contain many subsidiary figures. For example, the quartet on love by Phebe, Silvius, Orlando, and Rosalind (V.2.78–100) constitutes as a whole a logically-based figure (*Conglobatio*), the giving of a series of definitions for a single thing (what it is to love); at the same time, it is full of very obvious verbal patterns ('And so am I for Phebe' – 'And I for Ganymede' – 'And I for Rosalind' – 'And I for no woman'). The set-pieces in the play include witty debates, such as that of Celia and Rosalind on Fortune and Nature (I.2.30–54) and that of Corin and Touchstone on Court and Country (III.2.11–81); descriptions of events, such as Charles's wrestling with the three young men (I.2.110–22) and Orlando's battle with the lioness (IV.3.99–157); Jaques's moralisation on the dying stag (II.1.26–63), 'Seven Ages of Man' (II.7.140–67), and description of his melancholy (IV.1.10–18); Silvius's account of the behaviour of a lover (II.4.21–39), and Touchstone's parody of it (II.4.42–51); Rosalind's discourse on Time (III.2.299–322) and account of the marks of a man in love (III.2.358–68); and Touchstone's disquisition on the degrees of the lie (V.4.48–100). The large number of such set-pieces makes the style of the play as a whole leisurely and expansive rather than rapid and direct; the brilliant details give sparkle to the writing, but the overall effect is somewhat static, especially after the action has moved to Arden.

Imagery

In most of Shakespeare's plays there are recurrent words or groups of words which affect the atmosphere of the play and point to the themes which it is handling. Such recurrent words are often called *images*, even if they do not form part of a metaphor or other figure. Not surprisingly, *As You Like It* contains a large number of images relating to nature and to rural life. There are many references to animals (ape, ass, bell-wether, boar, cattle, cock-pigeon, cony, crow, doe, dog, ewes, fawn, goats, goose, hogs, ram, rat, sheep, weasel), to trees and plants (blossom, boughs, briers, bush, greenwood, holly, medlar, nut, oak, osiers), and to other sights of the countryside (brooks, corn-field, cottage, fields, harvest, and so on). These references help to build up a rural atmosphere in the play. There are also many references to weather (blow, foggy, freeze, frosty, ice, weather, wind) and to the seasons (April, December, May, months, seasons, springtime, winter), which have a similar function. The seasonal references also suggest the theme of *time*, which runs all through the play (age, day, harvest, hour, tomorrow, twelvemonth, year, yesterday); indeed, the word *time* itself is one of the commonest nouns in the play, occurring nearly fifty times. Other prominent word-clusters are the natural result of the story, for example ones dealing with family relationships (brother, daughter . . .), and with love. Among minor word-clusters can be noted one dealing with madness (lunacy, mad, madmen), and another (curiously enough) with the sea and sea-travel (Bay of Portugal, fathom, sea, south-sea, voyage).

Was the play written in haste?

There are a few things that suggest that *As You Like It* may have been written somewhat hurriedly. One is the handling of the exposition, the way in which information is given to the audience at the beginning of the play. It opens with Orlando giving Adam a long account of events of which the latter must already be fully aware, with no plausible reason suggested for this behaviour. Later in the scene, similarly, Charles tells Oliver all about the banishment of the old duke by the new duke, and the exiles in Arden, and the fact that Rosalind is still at court (I.1.93–112). This, Charles himself says, is 'old news' (I.1.93–4), and this is confirmed by the fact that Celia was 'too young' to appreciate Rosalind when these events took place (I.3.69), and by Duke Senior's reference to 'old custom' making their life in Arden tolerable (II.1.2). Both Orlando and Charles, therefore, give long and unmotivated accounts of earlier events, simply for the benefit of the audience.

There is also a structural point. In Shakespeare's theatre, a scene ended by the characters walking off; as they did so, the characters for the next scene entered by another door. It was therefore impossible for the same group of characters to end one scene and to begin the next, and the playwright had to plan the layout of the play so that this did not happen. But in *As You Like It* there appear to be two places where Shakespeare failed to do this advance planning. At the end of Act IV Scene 1, Celia and Rosalind go off to pass the time until two o'clock. But the next episode required by the story is precisely the one where Orlando fails to meet them at two o'clock, so Rosalind and Celia are required at the end of one scene and at the beginning of the next. Shakespeare solved the problem by inserting a short scene in between (IV.2); this scene contributes nothing to the plot; in it, Jaques and some lords come in, sing a song, and then go off again. Exactly the same situation arises at the end of Act V Scene 2, where Rosalind makes the arrangements for the great dénouement; Shakespeare gets round the difficulty in the same way again, by inserting a scene in which nothing happens except the singing of a song. Such improvisation suggests that the layout of the scenes had not been carefully worked out in advance. Moreover, a good deal else of what happens in Arden lacks plot: there is much padding-out with word-play, set-pieces, and generally 'stationary' material.

Moreover, there are some minor inconsistencies and carelessnesses. In one place Celia is said to be taller than Rosalind (I.2.261), but in another it is clearly implied that Rosalind is the taller (I.3.113). At the opening of the play, Orlando refers to his brother Jaques; later, however, we meet another character called Jaques, which is confusing for the audience; if Shakespeare had had time to polish the play, he would surely have removed the name *Jaques* from I.1.5. (When this brother of Orlando's comes in at the end of the play, he is referred to in the First Folio simply as 'Second Brother', not as 'Jaques'.)

There are, however, counter-arguments. Shakespeare's treatment of the exposition may be due, not to haste, but to a deliberate refusal to follow theatrical conventions: he is perhaps suggesting that having a natural-sounding exposition is a matter of no importance, and possibly even poking fun at contemporary theatrical attitudes. The absence of plot, similarly, may be deliberate choice: he is writing a play where the development of atmosphere and the deployment of themes matter more than a plot. What looks like structural improvisation may therefore be planned: the set-pieces and the bouts of wit are not excrescences, but on the contrary carry the main substance of what the play is saying. And the interpolated scenes, containing songs but no plot-element, are part of the technique of building up atmosphere rather than telling a story. As for the occasional carelessness and inconsistency, it could be argued that these occur in many of Shakespeare's plays, and that *As You Like It* is not worse than most. Alternatively, they can be explained as the result of revision: for example, whether Rosalind or Celia was the taller might have depended on the boys available for the parts at any given time, so that the text may well have been changed for a later production.

Part 4

Hints for study

General

You must know the play really well: read it time and time again. If you are asked a question about it, you should immediately be able to think of events or characters that help you to answer it, and to quote short passages from memory. If an extract from the play is placed in front of you, you should be able to identify it (who says it, what it is about, whereabouts in the play it comes, what happens next), and to explain any difficult words in it. When you write about the play, show that you know it well: support your argument by detailed reference to what happens in the play, and with short quotations. Read the play at different speeds: at first, you will sometimes want to work through it slowly, using the notes, to make sure that you understand everything; but remember that it is a play, so sometimes read it through without a break; and try to imagine it being acted as you read it, or even act it out yourself, reading aloud.

Secondly, you should *think* about the play. There are different views about what it means, what the main themes are, how Shakespeare gains his effects, and so on. In the end, you must decide what you think about these things. Obviously you want to know what other people have said about the play, and in Part 5 below there are some suggestions for further reading; but the final test for any view of the play is to be found in the text of the play itself. So when you are thinking or reading about the play, have the text open in front of you, and constantly check whether the view you are considering is borne out by what is said and done in the play. Do not make up your mind too quickly, or accept immediately the view of some critic; first weigh all the evidence that you can find in the play. It is especially necessary not to shut your eyes to evidence that contradicts your own current view. Indeed, unless you develop the habit of doing full justice to the evidence that contradicts your own view, you will not be *thinking* at all.

Thirdly, you must practise writing about the play. You need to be able to write simply and clearly, to arrange your material methodically, and to present evidence for your viewpoint. Sometimes you should write an essay at leisure, with the text of the play open in front of you. But if you are working for an examination, you should also practise writing essays under examination-conditions–in a limited time, and without the text of the play. Here are some suggestions for topics to study, followed by some essay-questions.

Topics for study

Examine Rosalind's behaviour (a) when she is dressed as a woman, (b) when she is dressed as a man. Does she talk and behave differently when she is in disguise?

Go through the play examining the attitudes to love which are expressed by different characters.

Look for evidence in the play which suggests that Touchstone is (a) an idiot, (b) intelligent and witty.

Analyse the character of (a) Jaques, (b) Adam, (c) Duke Frederick, (d) Duke Senior, (e) Phebe, (f) Celia, (g) Oliver. In each case, examine what the character says, what he or she does, and what other people say about him or her.

Examine the following scenes or episodes, and try to decide what (if anything) they contribute to the total effect of the play: (a) The account by two lords of Jaques moralising on the death of a deer (II.1.25–66); (b) Act II Scene 5; (c) Jaques's 'Seven Ages of Man' speech (II.7.140–67); (d) The debate between Touchstone and Corin on court life and country life (III.2.11–81); (e) Rosalind's disquisition on Time (III.2.294–322); (f) Act IV Scene 2; (g) Touchstone's account of 'a lie seven times removed' (V.4.66–100); (h) The masque of Hymen (V.4.105–43).

Try to describe the atmosphere which is built up in the scenes in the Forest of Arden. Look for the methods by which this atmosphere is produced.

Go through the play looking for references to (a) animals and birds, (b) trees, bushes, and plants, (c) gardens and gardening. What effect do these references have in the play?

Go through the play looking for incidents and speeches which introduce the themes of (a) liberty, (b) fortune, (c) nature. What do these themes contribute to the play?

Examine the presentation of rural characters in the play. To what extent is rural life either idealised or caricatured? Do William and Audrey resemble real country people?

Analyse the following speeches: (a) The first speech of Duke Senior (II.1.1–17); (b) Jaques's 'Seven Ages of Man' (II.7.140–67); (c) Phebe's speech beginning 'Think not I love him' (III.5.109–35). With each speech, examine the course of its argument, any changes of mood or tone or attitude that take place in it, the kinds of effect it produces, and the methods used to produce them (for instance particular metaphors or comparisons, rhetorical devices, dramatic irony).

Consider different possible interpretations of the title of the play.

Essay questions

If you have worked at the play in the ways suggested above, you should be able to tackle the following essay questions. They are arranged roughly in order of difficulty, and more elementary students are advised not to try the later ones.

1. What are the functions of the songs in *As You Like It*?
2. 'He uses his folly like a stalking-horse, and under presentation of that he shoots his wit' (Duke Senior). Is this a just assessment of Touchstone?
3. Give an account of the character and function of Jaques in *As You Like It*. What attitudes and events are there in the play which act as correctives or counterbalances to the views that he expresses?
4. Discuss the idea that, in *As You Like It*, people's characters change when they arrive at the Forest of Arden.
5. Examine the view that the central theme of *As You Like It* is the value of romantic love, and the ability of people to change themselves under its influence.
6. Discuss the contrast between Court and Country in *As You Like It*, and describe the methods by which this contrast is presented in the play.
7. What part is played in *As You Like It* by the contrast between Fortune and Nature?
8. Describe the methods by which, in *As You Like It*, Shakespeare builds up the distinctive atmosphere of the scenes set in the Forest of Arden.
9. '*As You Like It* derives much of its classical stability and poise from the fact that its plot barely exists. The comedy moves forward, not through a complex story line, . . . but simply through shifts in the groupings of characters. Their verbal encounters, their varying assessments of each other assume the status of events . . .' (Anne Barton). Discuss this view of the structure of *As You Like It*.
10. 'Shakespearian comedy is not finally satiric; it is poetic. It is not conservative; it is creative' (H. B. Charlton). Discuss this view with reference to *As You Like It*.
11. 'The "state of nature", as the play presents it, is as artificial, as remote from the true reality of the condition it purports to represent, as the "sophistication" which it replaces. Both, indeed, are instruments for asserting, within the limits of comedy, permanent truths about life which they do not directly or "realistically" reflect' (Derek Traversi). Discuss this view of *As You Like It*.

Writing an essay

When you write an essay, write about the subject set, and about nothing else. If you are asked a question on the character of Rosalind, do not discuss the life of Shakespeare, or sixteenth-century politics, or the Elizabethan stage: if you do, your examiner will just cross such passages out, and you will have wasted time and effort. Do not even take it for granted that your essay has to have some kind of introductory paragraph. Students are often taught that an essay must begin with an introduction and end with a conclusion; but this is not necessarily so, and the introductory paragraphs that students write are often mere padding. If you are asked to write an essay on the subject 'Does the character of Rosalind change when she moves from the Court to the Forest of Arden?', the best way to begin your essay is with some such words as 'At the beginning of the play, when she is at Court, Rosalind is . . .'; this gets you straight into the subject without fuss or waste of time. But before you begin, read the question carefully, and make sure you understand it; notice, for example, that essay-question number 8 above does not ask simply for a description of atmosphere; it asks you about the *methods* which Shakespeare uses for producing atmosphere, and that is quite a different question (including such things as recurrent images, and the use of songs).

Moreover, your essay must be planned. Do not start writing without thinking, but first jot down ideas. Then arrange these ideas under headings, which will provide the sections of your essay, and note down suitable examples or quotations under each heading. When you have the plan of the essay clear, begin writing. Try to write in a plain, straightforward way, but nevertheless with enthusiasm: an essay usually reads better if we feel that the writer is enjoying what he is talking about.

Specimen essay-plan

As an example of a simple plan for an essay, let us take the first essay-subject from our list, 'What are the functions of the songs in *As You Like It*?'. Thinking about the songs, we might jot down such ideas as 'pastoral atmosphere', 'jollity', 'weather', 'court and country', 'the seasons', 'hardships of rural life', 'filling gaps in action', together with examples and phrases from the songs. When we try to arrange the material, we might hesitate between two different schemes: one very simple plan would be just to take each song in turn, and say what functions it has; the alternative is to have a series of headings for different functions, illustrating each from the relevant songs.

If we were to adopt the second theme, we might produce a plan like the following: 1. Number and location of songs; 2. Structural functions; 3. Pastoral atmosphere; 4. Themes: Court and Country; 5. Themes: the seasons; 6. Ritual: the masque. When we came to write the essay, however, this plan might cause some difficulty: sections 3, 4, and 5 would be difficult to separate from one another, since in the songs the ideas are closely linked (for instance in lines like 'Blow, blow thou winter wind, Thou art not so unkind As man's ingratitude'). Sections 3 and 4 are especially intertwined, and it might be better to amalgamate them into a single section. Moreover, section 1 is not absolutely essential, and in a short essay it could well be omitted. This would give us a revised plan as follows: 1. Structural functions; 2. Pastoral atmosphere: Court and Country; 3. The seasons; 4. Ritual: the masque. In section 2 it might be convenient to deal with the first four songs of the play in turn, while in section 4 only the fifth song would be handled. To some extent, therefore, this final plan resembles the other scheme, in which each song is treated in turn.

Given our four main headings, we can then group under them the various ideas and examples that have been thought of, to give a more detailed plan. For example, section 1 might be expanded as follows:

1. Structural functions
   (a) Covering up repetition
       Orlando's story to Duke Senior.
   (b) Separating scenes
       Demands of Elizabethan stage (scene sequence)
       Resulting problem, and solution
       Examples: (i) 'What shall he have'
       (ii) 'It was a lover'

The plans for the other sections can be expanded similarly. Given the final plan, the essay can be made of various lengths, according to the amount of detail and illustrative material that is included. The following version is about nine hundred words long. Notice how use can be made of very short quotations from the play; this is especially useful in examinations.

Specimen essay

'What are the functions of the songs in *As You Like It*?' One of the functions of the songs in *As You Like It* is structural: some of them are used to cover up other action, and to provide time-intervals between scenes. 'Blow, blow' (II.7) is sung after Orlando has met Duke Senior, and during the song he tells the duke his history; the audience is thus spared a repetition of what it already knows. Moreover, the song provides a necessary period in which the starving Orlando and Adam can eat the food which has been offered to them.

Two of the songs provide necessary time-intervals between scenes. The Elizabethan stage had no front curtain: a scene ended by the characters walking off the stage, whereupon the next scene began by another group of characters walking on. It was thus hardly possible for a group of characters to go off at the end of one scene, and come on again immediately at the beginning of the next, supposedly some considerable time later. In two places Shakespeare prevents this from happening by inserting a very brief scene in which a song is sung. At the end of Act IV Scene 1, Rosalind and Celia arrange to meet Orlando two hours later, at two o'clock. But the very next episode required by the story is precisely the one where Orlando fails to keep this appointment at two o'clock. To separate the two scenes, and to bridge the time-interval, Shakespeare inserts the scene (IV.2) where Jaques and some lords sing 'What shall he have that killed the deer?'; this scene contributes nothing to the plot, and indeed nothing happens in it except the singing of the song. Exactly the same situation arises at the end of Act V Scene 2, where Rosalind arranges for Orlando, Silvius, and Phebe to meet her the following day. As before, Shakespeare solves the problem by inserting a short scene with a song (V.3): two pages sing 'It was a lover' to Touchstone and Audrey.

A more important function of the songs, however, is to create the feeling of country life, both its harshness and its joys, and especially to evoke an atmosphere of pastoral delight and rustic jollity. At the same time, because the contrast between Court and Country is a major theme of the play, the songs have a thematic function. Even the songs which make much of the 'winter wind' nevertheless contribute in their overall effect to a festive and happy atmosphere. 'Under the greenwood tree' (II.5) refers to 'winter and rough weather', but its general tenor is of the carefree joys of country life – the 'merry note' of the forester imitating 'the sweet bird's throat', the absence of enemies and ambition, the contentedness of the simple country life ('pleased with what he gets'). Jaques, however, improvises a third verse for the song, in which he says that the exiles are 'Gross fools' to abandon a life of 'wealth and ease' to come and live in Arden; and this reminds us that there is more than one view expressed in the play about the joys of rural life.

'Blow, blow, thou winter wind' (II.7) gives even more emphasis to the unkindness of the elements – the rude breath of the wind, the freezing sky, the waters blown up into waves – but nevertheless has the refrain 'Then hey-ho the holly, This life is most jolly', preferring rustic life to the ingratitude, feigning, and folly of the court. The reference to holly suggests Christmas, with its communal festivities and feasting and atmosphere of good will. The next song, 'What shall he have that killed the deer' (IV.2), is a rollicking huntsman's song, with a broad joke on the cuckold's horns; it evokes the mirth and companionship of rural life. Next comes 'It was a lover and his lass' (V.3), which evokes springtime in the country, with the 'green corn field', the 'acres of the rye', the lovers lying in the fields, and the birds singing in every stanza. It does indeed remind us that everything fades and dies, that human life 'is but a flower'; but the very image of the flower reinforces our sense of the richness of life in the spring, and suggests that we should 'take the present time', love and live fully while youth and spring are with us.

It will be noticed that there is a seasonal movement in the first four songs in the play: the first two give prominence to 'winter and rough weather'; the third is a jolly song without seasonal reference; and the fourth is a song about spring and youth. This sequence of songs suggests a movement from winter to spring, parallel to the change in the fortunes of the characters from adversity to prosperity.

'It was a lover', a joyous song of love and youth, occurs, very fittingly, just before the dénouement of the play, when the various lovers are finally to win their mates. The final song, 'Wedding is great Juno's crown' (V.4), forms part of that dénouement, and differs from the other songs in the play in that it forms part of the action. The first four songs contribute to theme and atmosphere, but they are not integrated in the action of the play. This final song, by contrast, is part of the masque of Hymen, which provides a formal and ritualistic resolution of problems and pairing off of lovers. As befits this context, the song is solemn, and does not handle the pastoral motifs found in the other songs; it celebrates wedlock, the 'blessed bond of board and bed', as the proper consummation of the loves and wooings with which the play has been concerned.

Part 5

Suggestions for further reading

The text

Line-references of *As You Like It* used in these Notes are taken from the New Penguin edition:

SHAKESPEARE, *As You Like It*, ed. H. J. OLIVER, Penguin Books, Harmondsworth, 1968.

Quotations in these Notes, however, are not necessarily identical with the text of Oliver's edition; in particular, the punctuation used is often nearer to that of the First Folio. The following editions of the play have full notes and long introductions:

SHAKESPEARE, *As You Like It*, (New Arden Series), ed. A. LATHAM, Methuen, London, 1975.

SHAKESPEARE, *As You Like It*, (New Shakespeare Series; often called the New Cambridge Series) ed. SIR A. QUILLER COUCH and J. D. WILSON, Cambridge University Press, 1926.

Collected works

SHAKESPEARE, *The Complete Works,* ed. P. ALEXANDER, Collins, London and Glasgow, 1951.

There are innumerable editions of Shakespeare's collected works. This is a convenient one-volume edition with a reliable text.

Critical works

HALIO, J. L., ed., *Twentieth Century Interpretations of As You Like It*, Prentice-Hall, Englewood Cliffs, New Jersey, 1968.

BROWN, J. R., ed., Shakespeare, *Much Ado About Nothing and As You Like It: a Casebook*, Macmillan, London, 1979.

These two books provide convenient collections of articles on the play. More advanced students will find sections or chapters on *As You Like It* in many other books about Shakespeare, especially in ones on the comedies. The following is a small selection:

BARBER, C. L., *Shakespeare's Festive Comedy*, Princeton University Press, Princeton, 1959.

BROWN, J. R., AND HARRIS, B., *Shakespearian Comedy: Stratford-upon-Avon Studies 14*, Edward Arnold, London, 1972.

CAMPBELL, O. J., *Shakespeare's Satire*, Gordian Press, New York, 1971.

CHARLTON, H. B., *Shakespearian Comedy*, Methuen, London, 1938.

HUNTER, G. K., *Shakespeare: the Late Comedies*, British Council and Longmans, London, 1962.

PALMER, J., *Comic Characters of Shakespeare*, Macmillan, London, 1946.

TRAVERSI, D., *An Approach to Shakespeare: Vol. I, Henry VI to Twelfth Night*, third edition, Hollis and Carter, London, 1968.

VICKERS, B., *The Artistry of Shakespeare's Prose*, Methuen, London, 1968.

SALINGAR, L. G., *Shakespeare and the Traditions of Comedy*, Cambridge University Press, Cambridge, 1974.

Deals with the various traditions of comedy which influenced Shakespeare.

CLEMEN, W., *The Development of Shakespeare's Imagery*, second edition, Methuen, London, 1977.

SPURGEON, C., *Shakespeare's Imagery*, Cambridge University Press, Cambridge, 1935.

Both discuss Shakespeare's imagery

GREG, W. W., *Pastoral Poetry and Pastoral Drama*, Bullen, London, 1906.

This gives a general history of pastoral literature in Europe.

HOTSON, L., *Shakespeare's Motley*, Rupert Hart-Davis, London, 1952.

WELSFORD, E., *The Fool*, Faber and Faber, London, 1935.

The first of these deals with the Elizabethan stage-fool, while the second is a general social and literary history of fools and jesters in Europe.

NOBLE, R., *Shakespeare's Use of Song*, Clarendon Press, Oxford, 1923.

Good on the use of songs in the plays.

Sources

BULLOUGH, G., *Narrative and Dramatic Sources of Shakespeare*, Vol. II, Routledge and Kegan Paul, London, 1958.

MUIR, K., *The Sources of Shakespeare's Plays*, Methuen, London, 1977.

For the play's sources consult the relevant portions of these two books.

Background works

TILLYARD, E. M. W., *The Elizabethan World Picture*, Chatto and Windus, London, 1943.

Gives an elementary account of the world-view of Shakespeare's time.

BARBER, C., *Early Modern English*, Deutsch, London, 1976.
An account of the English language in Shakespeare's time, and the ways in which it differed from present-day English.

GURR, A., *The Shakespearean Stage 1574–1642*, Cambridge University Press, 1970.
On the theatres, companies, actors, and stage-conditions of Shakespeare's time. This gives a very useful, though tightly-packed, account.

The author of these notes

CHARLES BARBER was educated at St Catharine's College, Cambridge where he won the Charles Oldham Shakespeare Prize. After a year's teacher-training at the University of London, where he won the Storey-Miller Prize for Educational Theory, he became a teacher at a London grammar school. During the war he served in the Royal Air Force; he then was lecturer in English at the University of Gothenburg, Sweden, assistant lecturer in English at the Queen's University of Belfast, and from 1959 to 1980 he was at the University of Leeds, where he was Reader in English Language and Literature, and Chairman of the School of English. His publications include an edition of Shakespeare's *Hamlet*, editions of three plays by Thomas Middleton, and a number of books on the English language, including a popular Pan paperback called *The Story of Language*.

YORK HANDBOOKS

The first ten titles

YORK HANDBOOKS form a companion series to York Notes and are designed to meet the wider needs of students of English and related fields. Each volume is a compact study of a given subject area, written by an authority with experience in communicating the essential ideas to students of all levels.

AN INTRODUCTORY GUIDE TO ENGLISH LITERATURE
by MARTIN STEPHEN

PREPARING FOR EXAMINATIONS IN ENGLISH LITERATURE
by NEIL McEWAN

AN INTRODUCTION TO LITERARY CRITICISM
by RICHARD DUTTON

THE ENGLISH NOVEL
by IAN MILLIGAN

ENGLISH POETRY
by CLIVE T. PROBYN

STUDYING CHAUCER
by ELISABETH BREWER

STUDYING SHAKESPEARE
by MARTIN STEPHEN *and* PHILIP FRANKS

ENGLISH USAGE
by COLIN G. HEY

A DICTIONARY OF LITERARY TERMS
by MARTIN GRAY

READING THE SCREEN
An Introduction to Film Studies
by JOHN IZOD